Organizational Readiness to e-Transformation

Organizational Readiness to e-Transformation

What preparations should organisations have in order
to be ready to transform into digital era?

Aqel M. Aqel

To order additional copies of this book, contact:
Xlibris Corporation
1-800-618-969
www.Xlibris.com.au
Orders@Xlibris.com.au
502512

Contents

Part Two   Organisational E-Readiness

List of Figures

To

My father who taught me ambition,

My mother who taught me dedication and commitment,

My wife and kids who always rose to my ambitions, and

To all who inspired my innovation.

PREFACE

The increasing dependency on information and communication technologies (ICT) resulted in new economic trends such as the digital economy phenomenon, which impacted many economic and social aspects in modern societies.

Transformation to new economic trends represented primarily by e-commerce was accompanied with an obvious public sector reforms under the title of electronic government (e-government). E-government is considered a continuation to public sector modernisation efforts that are mainly aimed at enhancing the operating environment in public sector.

The new economic trends contain great prosperous opportunities; at the same time it implied huge costs and serious risks. This book constructed a set of e-readiness levels that are global, regional, national, industry/business sector, organisational, community and personal readiness levels.

This book consists of two parts: Part I discusses e-readiness concepts, e-government definition, its benefits, barriers, and stages. E-readiness topic is then discussed from three perspectives – as a requirement, as a set of activities, and as an index; some globally accredited indices are illustrated to help reader understand its structures and components with some comments on its political values. Chapter three argues a classification for readiness layers which are global, regional, and national, and finally organisational readiness, which will be discussed further in part II of the book. Another classification for national readiness has been proposed, which consists of another six sub-levels.

Part II is fully focused on the organisational readiness. It will introduce a fully practical and auditable model for leaders to follow in order to assess their organisations' readiness to transform into smart organisations that use information technology (IT) effectively and efficiently.

Organisational e-readiness, which is a complimentary part of regional and global readiness; it argues the importance of e-readiness assessment in a structured and quantitative way that contain relevant and valid criteria to assess readiness within organisations from various and balanced perspectives. The proposed organisational e-readiness model which is more focused on public sector agencies consists of five interrelated categories; these are strategy, business process, technology, changeability, and ICT security.

These intersected and tightly related tracks outline key pillars for any ICT based transformation; in simple words, a business unit or even a public sector agency needs clear strategic direction, which will support reformulation of strategy derived business processes to be enabled using technology by its wide means; if these three factors are ready, the organisation needs a change supportive environment like managed risks and sincere leadership in order to carry it out successfully. Due to the criticality of information security, it is receiving high concerns from stakeholders and already classified as one of the barriers for e-government transformation; security in its comprehensive meaning consists of confidentiality, integrity, and availability of information that supports business process within organisation; this mandates various roles and activities to be maintained by organisations.

Finally, the book aims to answer the question 'what preparations should government agencies have in order to be ready to implement e-government concepts and services'.

Author

Part One:

Introduction to E-transformation

CHAPTER ONE

Introduction

Chapter Summary

This chapter will help you establish a fair understanding about book's topic; interesting information has been gathered and summarised from various sources about e-government concepts, benefits, various approaches, and key barriers. This will help the reader outline e-readiness topic.

Different e-readiness perspectives will be summarised out from reviewed literature in preparation for the conclusion of e-readiness levels and criteria; these are e-readiness as a requirement, e-readiness as an activity, and e-readiness as an index.

1.1 E-government Definition

THE term e-government is relatively new and has been used heavily in the last decade, basically to describe the effective use of ICT in government agencies activities; there is some dispute on the e-government definition as we have differences in 'scope, government structure, budget allocations, resources, availability of skills and technology, and central government vision' (AOEMA, 2007).

The term was expanded later to mean more than this basic meaning as various e-government experiments results in a more in-depth understanding of the topic and its relationships with established sciences, for example, politics, economy, jurisdiction, and management.

E-government initiatives also produced many changes in societies, which went into this experiment politically, economically, and socially.

Gartner Group described e-government as 'the continuous optimization of service delivery, constituency participation, and governance by transforming internal and external relationships through technology, the Internet and new media' (Gascó, 2007).

The office of management and budget (OMB) defined e-government as 'Government's use of IT (such as Wide Area Networks, the Internet, and mobile computing) to exchange information and services with citizens, businesses, and other arms of government' (OMB, 2007). e-government concept is not only concerned with transactional service level of government body, but many authors realised the transformational impact of e-government which stimulates the need to expand the e-government concept; this is considered relatively new as e-government is in its initial stage of development (AOEMA, 2007).

Electronic government initiatives include changing the inside of public-sector organizations (what has been called 'back-office adjustments'), improving service delivery, and promoting participation and democracy (often referred to as e-governance or e-democracy). (Gascó, 2007, p. 684)

Booz Allan and Hamilton (BA&H) called for a new understanding and suggested 't-government' to describe the new stages of e-government which is expected to be the concluding stage of the automated public sector reached by societies who experienced relatively successful e-government programmes over the past decade (BA&H, 2005).

T-government is about transforming government into new reforms based on ICT rather than just changing services channels from conventional service channel (mainly face to face and regular mail system) to new kinds of remote service delivery. In the initial stages of e-government initiatives, agencies experienced two levels of automation in their services: first, automating strategic services they introduce – wherever applicable, and second, using ICT to facilitate supportive administrative operations. This is depending on the digitisation ability of perspective strategic services or what is described as 'bittability' (BA&H, 2005), in addition to some other readiness factors; For example, actual transportation services may not be digitised; on the contrary, full business cycle of tax payment is a clear example for an automated strategic service. t-Government is about transformation, changing fundamentally the way government does what it does. It is more than moving services online; it will derive full comprehensive internal and external changes in government agency and its relationships with all stakeholders, for example, constituents, federal government, peer agencies, private sector, and so on.

This transformational change needs to be led by business needs and should satisfy stakeholders' benefits while maintaining governance role of government agencies as they are responsible for legality and authority.

Agencies traditionally practiced power and control within societies according to various degrees and shapes of democracy. Current technologies mandated new practices of power and relationships, which makes e-government much wider than electronic system as it seriously touches the way government is governing societies.

Before discussing political, economic, and social relationships with e-government in order to specifically discuss its impacts on e-readiness assessment, which this book is all about, first of all, I would like to shed some light on the evolution of e-government and its common models.

Historically, public sector used IT products like computers, databases, networks, and so on to store and manipulate information in their daily work. Government agencies, as many other sectors, witnessed waves of managerial development. Heeks argued that 'ICTs are usually used to automate the internal workings of government by processing data, whereas in more modern public administrations, they support and transform the external workings of governance by processing and communicating data' (Heeks, 2001, pp. 4–6).

The evolution of Internet which triggered e-commerce due to the huge potential business opportunities have influenced agencies to start e-government initiative which followed e-commerce step in its initial forms and techniques (Carsten, 2005); this is evident by one simple fact that same citizens who are dealing with private sector e-commerce portals to order products and services are the same people who need to visit public sector agencies to receive services.

1.2 E-government Stages

Reviewed literature referenced a model of four stages suggested by Gartner Group in 2000, which consists of four main stages to reform e-government sector in order to be fully Web enabled and to be more constituent oriented rather than process oriented (Baum and Maio, 2000).

The model basically consists of four stages as follows:

Phase 1 – Presence: Agency will create a static website that shows information about agency, publish news about its services, give instructions about services, and print/download service requests forms and instructions. Almost all e-government programmes can manage to afford this stage with minimal readiness.

Phase 2 – Interaction: Agencies will build websites that provide search capabilities, offer dynamic forms to fill and submit online, and facilitate linkage to other related websites. One example is unified e-government access. It may offer online and/or offline communication with consular. Online collaboration and information exchange will be afforded after integrating back-end systems. Definitely, this level mandates extra level of readiness technically and managerially.

Phase 3 – Transaction: In this stage, in addition to information and instructions, agencies offer complete e-service transactions that starts by filling and validating online service requests, complete services remotely or semi remotely, receive feedback by electronic means, for example, email or mobile. Electronic integration between agencies will be enforced to reduce constituents' time and efforts by fully depending on integrated networks. In fact 'this is the current stage for several agencies and the most immediate target for many e-government initiatives worldwide' (Baum and Maio, 2000).

Phase 4 – Transformation: Passing through the previous stages successfully will lead agencies to have more transparency with constituents as they reached to fully integrated and unified systems; transformation stage will be technically achievable if supported politically and socially.

In this stage, government agencies will have new optimised processes that satisfy both agency business requirement and governance objectives. In this stage, shared authentic electronic identity, secured electronic document exchange, and electronic financial settlement need to be provided at national or regional level; in addition to dependable information and telecommunication infrastructure that afford high availability are considered an essential readiness factor.

This stage will involve high internal business processes optimisation; for example, most agencies share certain functions pertaining to federal relationships. Unified portals to serve internal and cross-agencies activities will yield a lot of uniformity and centralisation in processing common activities.

Examples of such services may include human resources management processes and unified procurement and tendering systems across agencies; such services are expected to reduce agency level efforts on non-strategic activities and will allow agencies to concentrate on strategic ones.

In this stage, there are many social and managerial impacts. 'This phase will also include the development of state-of-the-art intranets that can link government employees who work in different agencies. Governmental transformation will also include the design of extranets that allow the seamless flow of information and collaborative decision-making among federal, state and local government agencies; private and not-for-profit sector partners; and the public' (Baum and Maio, 2000).

This was the visionary model of e-government that was common after 2000. There was no evidence in the reviewed literature about how long each stage lasts as it varies according to many factors; BA&H (2005) suggested an enhanced model in their report titled 'Beyond e-government'; they appended Gartner four-phases model after monitoring real experiences in e-government field; the report described four waves; the last two describe transformational phases to 't-government'.

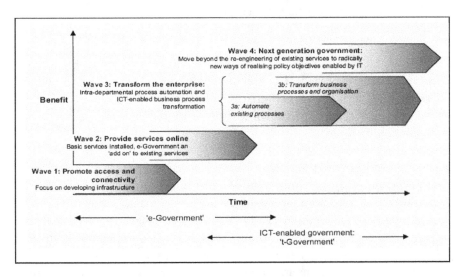

Figure 1.1: The evolution of e-government.
Source: Booz Allan and Hamilton, 'Beyond e-government – the world's most technology enabled transformations', 2005.

As indicated in figure 1.1, four waves of evolution are experienced by most e-government programmes. Actually, each wave requires different implementation readiness; for example, technical readiness for first wave may be limited to offering website hosting and Internet connectivity, while waves three and four need high ICT availability and matured security; stage two impacts on business process is much less than later stages that will definitely mandate huge change management efforts due to its political and social consequences.

In all waves, potential benefits of implementations continue to derive motivation and facilitate financing decisions. As we early noted, early initiatives were highly influenced by private sector e-commerce initiatives, mainly to achieve high customer satisfaction and reduced transaction costs which yield new ways for differentiation to pioneers. This formed a pressure on public sector to follow. I will be clarifying this in the next section as I will discuss benefits of e-government from various perspectives.

1.3 E-government Benefits

Before e-government initiatives, there were lots of calls for public sector modernisation and development; many authors described the opportunities that IT is promising to provide to public sector development; for example, Barton in 1979 argued that 'the introduction of new public management was an attempt to modernise "old type" bureaucracy seen as static, dysfunctional, and unable to adapt to changing circumstances' (Barton, 1979, pp. 28–29).

E-government programmes could be considered as a continuation to such efforts, due to the benefits ICT succeeded to deliver. ICT also lead to political and social effects: 'electronic commerce applications in the public sector might lead to efficiency gains and enhanced trust from its citizens in government' (Wyman et al., 1997).

Benefits of e-government are many, yet it is hard to assess in order to prove effectiveness and efficiency; some consider users' satisfaction as the key indicator. 'User satisfaction has been proposed as the most useful surrogate measure of system success' (Galletta et al., 1989), hence democratic governments are working seriously to get more trust and satisfaction to constituents. Wyman et al. in 1997 argued that 'electronic commerce applications in the public sector might lead to efficiency gains and enhanced trust in government from its citizens' (Wyman et al., 1997).

In addition to satisfaction, cost optimisation was always a determinant factor in evaluating efficiency, otherwise developing and operating new electronic services channels may become a burden on the agency; the following graph by BA&H in 2005 describes how total cost to serve is increased in the beginning and then lowered while enforcing new channel utilisation and gradually enhancing its effectiveness:

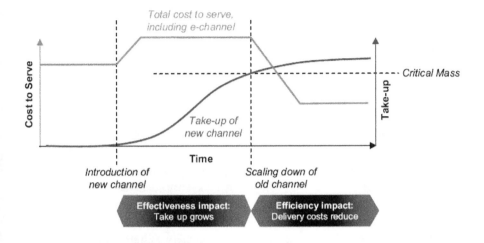

Figure 1.2: Phases of impact during introduction of a new channel.
Source: Booz Allan and Hamilton, 'Beyond e-government – the world's most technology enabled transformations', 2005.

United Nations' World Public Sector Report (2003) stated that 'Internal Revenue Service (IRS) processes 112 million individual tax returns and 79 million (m) business tax returns. It also file 1.5 billion information returns of individuals and businesses combined make 65 million payments totaling almost U.S. $2 trillion. In 2003, 53 million individual and small business, tax returns and 500 million information returns were filed electronically. The IRS collected U.S. $1.6 trillion electronically. The IRS website received 4 billion hits and 500,000 forms were downloaded' (WPSR, 2003).

The above statistics about IRS indicate the huge potential saving on national economy from transaction cost, which is not easy to estimate. The cost of constituent's trip to agency, cost of waiting in a queue in order to be served will certainly encounter a lot of saving.

'One example is the UK's Driver and Vehicle Operators (DVO) group, where ICT related efficiency improvements have enabled savings of £1.4m (€2.1m) in 2004–5' (WPSR, 2003).

'Italy reports annual cost savings of €90m, Sweden €2.7m, USA US$132m (€110m), and Canada CAN$12m (€8.5m). Automation of back office processes has also dramatically speeded up service delivery in many countries' (BA&H, 2005).

There are also examples of significant time savings for customers; 'in the USA, e-Gov Benefits has reduced processing time by 90 per cent to a little around five minutes! Efficiency gained to government through IT enablement are beginning to be realised in a number of countries – Canada has been able to reduce the number of processing staff by 40 per cent, enabling them to be reallocated to customer facing roles. Back-office automation has led to savings of up to €750,000 for the Federal Office of Economics and Export Control in Germany' (BA&H, 2005).

The above figures also indicate the increased trust ability of e-government services as far as it can offer better performance and customer satisfaction.

Political and leaders are continually managing to reduce bureaucracy in government agencies, and promote treating constituents as customers and offering them services twenty-four seven. This was evidenced by the managerial revolution in public sector management, especially in democratic countries characterised by business process optimisation and automation, quality systems implementation, cut-offs, and privatisation. This revolution was due to various political and social pressures. In fact, these initiatives leveraged public sector readiness to embrace new e-commerce concepts in delivering service; for example, agencies who manage to build back-end systems and re-engineer internal business processes are more ready to successfully operate online services; I will discuss this with more details in chapter two 'Readiness Criteria'. But now, let us discuss barriers to e-government.

1.4 Barriers to E-Government

The promising and convincing benefits of e-governments are faced by a set of barriers; Literature discussed many barriers to e-government implementation. These barriers need to be examined as it will help to understand e-readiness and conclude an assessment model.

Many thinkers discussed the barriers from various perspectives; some focused on the technology itself, while others discussed barriers from the automation programmes perspectives. Managing automation programmes passed into an accelerated learning curve in the last few decades where many development and implementation mythologies were evolved revealing that project management capabilities is essential in any organisational change.

Ebrahim and Irani (2005) in their research about barriers to information systems infrastructure development categorised some barriers illustrated with practical examples in the following domains:

1. Technical Infrastructure
2. Funding/Financing
3. Leadership

4. Strategic Management
5. Security
6. Other barriers

As e-government concept expanded to include many other aspects which exceed organisation's scope of authority to include national and probably regional/ international considerations, I would like to restructure barriers to the following domains:

1. Technology related barriers.
2. Cultural/Societal barriers.
3. Organisational barriers.

I think this classification will help leaders and thinkers address any barriers and assign responsible stakeholders to deal with it. Early studies discussed the criticality of ICT related infrastructural barriers like access to public networks and the affordability of integrated information in highly available database management systems. for example, a study by Harvard and IBM in the early of 21st century titled 'The readiness to network world' was so focused on the technology. Later studies realised the criticality of other social and political barriers. Wenbo (2002) argued that few studies realised the role of organisational factors, for example, leadership style and strategic planning for websites. He concluded that 'There is no strong theoretical base for predicting how these factors influence the success of electronic government commerce' (Wenbo, 2002).

Another non-technical barrier is that skilled workers in various technology tracks may prefer to work for for-profit sectors; this creates extra barrier as federal roles may lack human resources motivation and retention policies. This emphasises the importance of aligning e-government programme with other economic and human capital development programmes.

I will be discussing each of the mentioned categories and point up some examples; this exercise will help us in concluding our organisational e-readiness model.

1.4.1 Technology Related Barriers

Technology related barriers are factors that pertain to the nature of technology itself. Scalable physical infrastructure is one key capacity that many nations lack; especially in developing countries where they fail to early establish public switched telephone networks (PSTN), which later transformed into digital networks, and become the basis for digital infrastructure.

Technology itself – digital products such as databases and programmed systems and digital exchange protocols – is continually developing and maturing up; it just needed time to become stabilised and near perfect. Software developers need to balance its sophistication with many factors such as existing affordable computing power by consumers and manageability factors. It is clear for many who watch hardware and software development over the past years that both was evolving in parallel, not forgetting economic market considerations such as return on investment in technology, short life time of service in front of capitals invested in the technology and the overwhelming risks of absoluteness.

Everybody experienced the low performance of newly launched systems on the existing machines and the non-stop demand for upgrade which mandated migration to a new scalable platform. I can consider the investment in people to help them shift to the new technologies and scarcity issues are technology related factors.

Shifting from MS-Windows box servers to a Unix server might be a nightmare for many data centers; it will mandate some staff replacement which for sure will incur extra costs. The whole upgrade project is threatened by lots of risks unless done with qualified resources and planned efforts.

Finally, I can add technical security issues to the set of technology barriers, yet security is not limited to technology factors. It is much wider and will be discussed later. Technology is still vulnerable to various threats by nature; I think such kinds of barriers will continue to exist as it is part of the long struggle between good and bad. New developments and enhancements will keep bringing new threats, but as far as risks are affordable and manageable, it will not prevent societies' transformation towards e-government; it will hinder it for a certain time which varies from one society to another as well as from one firm to another.

Risk appetite is culture related. Societies are supposed to address security barriers and consider it seriously in their national transformation programmes – not to eliminate it, as this seems to be impossible, but to minimise it to manageable levels.

We can cluster technology barriers in the following categories:

1. Hardware related barriers.
2. Connectivity barriers
3. Software barriers
4. Technology management barriers
5. Technical security barriers

1.4.2 Cultural and Societal Barriers

One key barrier to implement e-gov is the lack of funding which could be solved by adopting long-term private-public partnerships to develop and implement e-government.

According to the e-government survey of 2000 conducted in the USA by the International City/County Management Association and Public Technology, Inc., over 50 per cent of government organisations that responded to the e-government survey indicated that lack of financial resources is a main barrier to adopting an e-government initiative for a public sector organisation (Norris et al., 2001).

Countries which lack major infrastructural resources may build service level agreements with qualified private sector contractors to either build special solutions or use their ready resources based on partnership models; in fact the ability to build service level agreement is another organisational barrier which we will discuss in the next chapter about e-readiness.

In some countries no clear legislation are in place to cover such engagements between sectors or facilitate external investors' involvement. This crystallises one key barrier to be characterised as legal barriers.

Cultural factors also include the relationships between individuals and government agencies. Each country has its own structure of relationships between government as a governing party and nations. Various democratic and authoritarian regimes were built over years and built with them their own cultural barriers. In fact, this makes e-readiness harder to standardise when it comes to non-technical issues.

Constituents' ability to utilise existing technology is another barrier; for example, many nations suffer from illiteracy. Recently, many education specialists defined a new kind of illiteracy – digital illiteracy. United Nations declares that digital gap is one of the global threats that challenge leaders; not only in the developing and Third World countries but importantly in the leading developing countries as it is responsible to bridge this gap by extensive education and knowledge sharing programmes. Such programmes are considered long-term investment for leading technology manufacturers to sustain market expansions for their technology products.

Many e-readiness models which discussed nations' readiness argued the role of central or federal government ability to support the transformation.

We can cluster cultural and societal barriers in the following key factors:

1. Government structures and relationships.
2. Community barriers to consume technology.

1.4.3 Organisational Barriers

Who should lead e-government initiative in agencies? This was a challenging question for many programmes; it could be classified as part of the organisational readiness. Many case studies reported the failure of initiatives led by ICT functions, especially those who have limited representation in top management; some of these initiatives also failed to cascade the required motivated change upward to top management or other departments; the lesson learned is that change agent need to be in a high position of agency organisation structure in order to be able to lead such initiatives. This emphasises the importance of ICT function empowerment and involvement in business level issues; in fact ICT function has a set of readiness criteria in order to be ready to play different roles in e-gov implementation; we may classify these roles to include the pure conventional role of technology custodian and other managerial and leadership roles that will add value to the e-gov programme.

The contribution of information and communication technologies to what has been called the 'reinvention' of government depends, precisely, on the degree of reform a particular government has fulfilled. Thus, the role (and therefore the importance) of technology is different in each stage of the public-sector modernisation process. (Gascó, 2007)

Gascó argued that '[a]s governments become more citizen-oriented (and as such, usually more efficient, transparent, and accountable), they adopt more information and communication technologies in their interactions with citizens' (Gascó, 2007).

As e-government projects exceed usual technology projects, it needs special leadership to support it fully and disseminate required enthusiasm to key stakeholders in order to convert dreams into realities.

Wenbo (2002) argued that comprehensive changes mandated by e-government stages require the transformational leadership style which is mainly characterised by vision, strategy, and influence. 'The transformational leader, in contrast, is visionary, willing to take risks and highly adaptable to change. In addition to that, the transformational leader draws on many qualities to perform effectively and exemplifies the values, goals and culture of the organisation while being highly aware of environmental factors affecting the organisation.' Moreover, the transformational leader is willing to delegate authority and builds subordinates' skills and confidence rather than dominates subordinates' (Wenbo, 2002).

Transformational leadership is defined as 'the process of influencing major changes in the attitudes and assumptions of organisation members and building commitment for major changes in the organisation's objectives and strategies'(Evcimen, 2006).

As government body consists of a set of agencies and departments, leadership of e-government programmes is needed also at federal and national levels rather than agency level in order to provide enough support to transformation progression including reforming agencies' intersected processes in order to successfully change long years of standard formulations that government agencies usually adhering to by the power of legitimacy.

Introducing serious changes will always be faced by resistance from stakeholders especially in firms with established bureaucracy; constituents themselves may feel uncertain regarding the new digital ways of delivering services. This resistance is expected to be higher in the first stages of transformation.

Transformational leadership will help pursue stakeholders to adopt and customise new practices of power and control; it will give enough support to stakeholders to creatively utilise technology in public sector to comply with e-government targets stated by leaders.

Strategic Management

Parallel with transformation leadership, many authors recognised two factors about transformational leadership style and the strategic planning in organisations. Strategic planning in corporate level and IT levels are affecting the way management is going to deal with e-government initiative; I think those who practice strategic planning are ready to adopt organisational change such as implementing new ways to introduce services to constituents. For example, technology today can give chances to reengineer services, and strategic planning will raise risks earlier as it includes PEST and SWOT analysis, which will raise technology impacts and change drivers through the periodic assessment of internal and external pressures.

Lack of effective strategic planning is another key barrier to e-government; strategic planning can help in managing change through the following ways:

1. Developing a clear sense of mission and desired service outcomes,
2. Helping the agency understand the views of its stakeholders and clients,

3. Encouraging an organisational culture of innovation and flexibility, and
4. Linking agency strategies with performance measures (Berry, 2007).

Strategic planning at community levels such as county or national is much more sophisticated than private sector planning, as there are many stakeholders with diverse interests. This places more responsibility on the leaders of change in gathering diverse stockholders' efforts and employ them in the right direction.

E-government initiative touches almost all agencies at the county or national level; this adds an extra level of complication in order to formulate effective strategies that serve all agencies' interests while maintaining simplicity and practicality.

Such plans mandate holistic strategic planning process in order to incorporate various stakeholders' needs and conclude a doable high level strategy on various aspects, for example, infrastructure, integration, shared business process, etc.

Strategic management is the recommended style of management that incorporates performance management in the operational level to assess strategies and help implementing strategic plans.

E-government initiatives must promote strategic planning and management as part of the readiness in order to effectively manage the investments in technology and human resources mandated by the e-government programmes; for example, in the absence of strategic management at agency level, how agency will be able to assess the effectiveness and performance of lunched e-services, or how it will be ready to prioritise key business processes that directly affect agency strategy and postpone those which does not directly support agency strategy.

Parallel with strategic management, many agencies lack the ability to manage performance. In fact, performance management is a key readiness criterion as it will give trust to e-government programmes. Federal government and tax payers will feel comfortable to finance e-government initiatives as far as there programmes is governed by effective performance management systems.

Agency experience in performance management will be reflected on effectively prioritising, developing, and managing e-services in the early stages of the programmes.

Security

Many ICT professionals noted the increased understanding of the role of security and privacy of managing IT by many firms; it is believed that this came after the Internet; security consists of a triangular concept known as the 'CIA' – confidentiality, integrity, and availability (ITGI, 2005).

Security and privacy contains many organisational aspects rather than technical aspects, for example, data classification, security policies and strategies, disaster recovery and business continuity, which will formulate and direct the technical aspects of security.

Authentication and privacy increasingly became an issue in modern e-government models as initial models did not raise serious security implications as it was based on one-way communication during the Web presence stage of e-government.

While integrity and availability of information may look more hardware and software related and could be categorised as infrastructural readiness, confidentiality of information forms a concern for all stakeholders in e-government programmes.

Government agencies need to balance between the contradicting issues that they face naturally while embarking on e-government initiatives which form a cyclical risk to the whole initiative such as

- the increased data sharing and transparency of information and
- the need to practice control while authenticating processes and constituents which is one of the reasons for agencies existence in the first place.

In authentication perspective of integrity, Holden and Millett (2005), argued the implications of the typical relationships between citizens and agencies, for example, long-term intermittent relationship with private sector may hinder agencies from adopting unified authentication and privacy policies; on the contrary, e-authentication mechanisms between agencies and federal government is a requirement for successful e-gov and must be addressed at national or regional levels with smart dynamic solutions that suit everybody; e-authentication forms a governmental responsibility to authenticate persons and firms exactly as in manual system. We need to bear in mind that government agencies may be the only parties that have the right to introduce authentication service for individuals and organisations in most countries; for example, some papers need to be stamped and authenticated from concerned government agencies in order to be accepted.

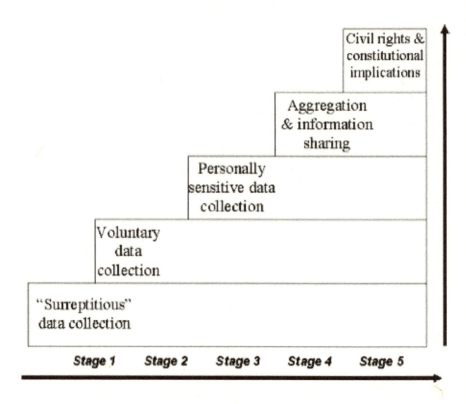

Figure 1.3: Level of data collection and related privacy concerns.
Source: Hiller and B´elanger (2001), from Holden and Millett (2005).

Figure 1.3 illustrates the relationship between e-government maturity and potential privacy implications. In stage 3 and above, the following major security issues may form a barrier to the implementation of e-government:

1. **Authentication** of parties and information: validation of the identity of stakeholder who provided the information or action.
2. **Non-repudiation**: Sender cannot deny sending an electronic message.
3. **Privacy**: intended or unintended access of information by unauthorised parties; this is the major reason that many parties may feel reluctant to pass information online.
4. **Availability:** maintaining up and running systems 24/7 incur lots of technical and managerial efforts.

Despite the fact that technical solutions were provided to cover the above-mentioned issues, yet most countries have limitations; it could be summarised in the following:

- **Different understandings of security**: perception of security and privacy is culturally related and has been evolved differently in societies – for example, some societies have legislations concerning privacy and disclosure of information. Not only does this raise the awareness of security issues but also creates compliancy requirements to e-government programmes; for example, the Privacy Impact Assessment act (PIA) by Office of Budget and Management (OMB) in 2002 mandated periodic analysis of how information is handled; it aims to

  (i) ensure handling conforms to applicable legal, regulatory, and policy requirements regarding privacy,
  (ii) determine the risks and effects of collecting, maintaining, and disseminating information in identifiable form in an electronic information system, and
  (iii) examine and evaluate protections and alternative processes for handling information to mitigate potential privacy risks (Holden and Millett, 2005).

  OBM also realised the criticality to reconduct a privacy impact assessment (PIA) when changes to an information system create new privacy risks.

  Many countries still need to embark on developing legislative frameworks for security in order to build and customise security infrastructures.

- **Lack of national and regional security infrastructure**: such as public key infrastructure (PKI) and its implementation. Digital signature was proposed as an effective solution to privacy, authentication and non-repudiation issues, yet it needed preparations at national levels with customised solutions which designed to suit various beneficiaries' needs, for example, corporate and individuals.
- Security is an ongoing risk associated with most of the IT projects. In terms of e-government, the degree of risk escalates as the use of public networks increases (Medjahed et al., 2003, from Ebrahim and Irani, 2005).
- Existing security countermeasures will be obsolete within a few years of use; for example, the symmetric digital encryption system (DES) of 128 bit was effective for a period of time. Then it became ineffective as new computing machines like Pentium personal computers were able to crack it within hours; this creates the challenge of continuously developing enhanced security solutions, which bear to be a limitation for many countries.

Other Barriers

There are other technical and organisational barriers, like managing the people impact of ICT enabled transformation which could be related to leadership readiness that use effective change management programmes that address key risks of transformation and identify dynamic plans to mitigate these risks.

In the next chapter, I will discuss various readiness criteria, categorise it from different perspectives based on e-government stage intended, and taking into consideration key barriers discussed.

CHAPTER TWO

E-Readiness Concepts

Chapter Summary

In this chapter, readiness topic will be introduced. It will be defined and analysed from various perspectives. e-readiness will discussed as a prerequisite for huge technology programmes in order to measure risks; also it will be discussed as an activity that needs planning, execution, and controlling like any project, and finally, it will be discussed as indices that used to rank countries' abilities to implement and transform to new public reforms that support economic and social development.

2.1   Definition

T HE term e-readiness sounds fully compatible with the wave of new terms that address electronic age like e-commerce, e-learning, e-health, etc. In reviewed literature the term sometimes was followed by the word 'assessment' to describe wide domains and approaches of measurements to assess capacity to participate or transform into electronic age.

E-readiness measures how well a society is positioned to utilise the opportunities provided by Information and Communication Technologies (ICT). (Ojo et al., 2007)

There are various domains to assess e-readiness, in addition to various levels of sophistication; for instance, managers in a certain firm may need to know if they are ready to start an e-commerce initiative or not yet. They may wonder what factors are affecting this readiness and the weight of criticality of each factor.

On the other hand, leaders in societies are discussing e-readiness on national or regional levels; they may need an answer for a set of questions:

- Do our people have the capacity to use electronic channels in order to collaborate with launched e-services?
- Do our legislative systems have provisions to handle electronic transactions' consequences?
- Do we have dependable electronic payment system?
- Do our workers have the skills needed to practice business in the digital age?

The above-mentioned questions and many other ones are reflecting the significance of readiness to electronic age, or networked age as some resources call it; these questions as well indicate that readiness exceeds pure technical issues as e-readiness apparently integrated to various political, economic, legislative, and social issues.

In general, e-readiness is 'the degree to which an economy or community is prepared to participate in the digital economy . . . readiness profile is composed of national policies, level of technology integration, and regulatory practices' (APEC, 2000).

As this book is concerned with readiness to e-government, I will quote United Nations' public sector report's (WPSR) definition for the e-readiness:

> E-readiness is the generic capacity or aptitude of the public sector to use ICT for encapsulating public services and deploying to the public high quality information (explicit knowledge) and effective communication tools that support human development. (WPSR, 2003, p. 135)

The definition clearly addressed six key elements of e-readiness:

Generic capacity: E-readiness should assess attributes that are shared by and is common to all or most stakeholders. It should be prominently needed for the desired transformation; readiness attributes or criteria need to be as objectively measurable as possible in order to be able to accurately assess and follow up readiness progress.

Use ICT: This clearly states that e-readiness is about technology where the main driver is the advancements in ICT, which provide new means to communicate and conduct business. The word 'use' emphasises human and organisational involvement in technology. This exemplifies the other non-technical aspects of e-readiness.

Public Service: Readiness should be concerned with factors that assist agencies in delivering better public value which conventionally expressed as services. Public value does not necessarily mean transform current services into Web enabled, probably to reduce cost of transactions for instance; this for sure is one of the objectives, but e-government may extend its pubic value by using ICT to provide more participation of constituents in democratic process, for example, decision making and identifying priorities which will result in more trust in government bodies and will lead to national prosperity.

High Quality Information: WPSR in the 2003 definition realised the importance of information which could be classified as a key service that public sector should cater for. A survey conducted in 2002 among United States' non-online users who assumed that at some point in future they would go online; 30 per cent of them saw it as an opportunity to conduct a general search for information, while 60 per cent of online users were using it for that purpose, specifically searching for jobs and training courses (WPSR, 2003, p. 64).

Parallel with e-services, agencies need to address ability to provide information when assessing readiness which will be used to build their e-government strategic plans; this may raise the question about what information agencies need to provide.

Communication Tools: Readiness to communicate better is a core e-readiness part; tools include the Internet, the Intranet, email, SMS, phones, mobile, wireless networks, etc. This justifies why telecommunication infrastructure forms a major share of the quantitative readiness index as we will discuss later.

Reviewed results of e-readiness indices revealed that countries with less ready telecom infrastructure always fall down in the ranking list. They will not be able to transform into e-government simply because they lack the apparatus of communication. Even if they manage to provide e-services, their transformation programmes will suffer from low usage. This makes many e-government programmes delay their transformation initiatives until they reach better telecom readiness. By the time they are more prepared, they may suffer from extra digital divide. This also justifies why many countries liberate telecom sectors.

Human Development: If e-government fails to enhance human life, then it is useless; WPSR classifies three types of e-government:

1. **Wasteful** – engages resources but does not result in optimisation of government operations.

2. **Pointless** – even if it optimises government operations, it has no (or only minimal) effect on the development objectives preferred by society.
3. **Meaningful** – optimises government operations, and
    - supports human development, that is, empowers people, raises human capabilities;
    - equips people for genuine participation in the inclusive political process;
    - supports values considered as essential for human development in the twenty-first century (WPSR, 2003, p. 10).

2.2 E-readiness Perspectives

Away from the mentioned definition, we need to differentiate a few intersected usages of the term 'e-readiness' which are as follows: e-readiness as a requirement, e-readiness as an activity, and e-readiness as an index.

In the following sections, I will provide a brief description for each perspective.

2.2.1 E-readiness As a Requirement

Basically, e-readiness was understood as a requirement in order to countermeasure various risks incorporated in technology programmes which are usually funded by national budgets, that is, tax payers' money. 'There is an opportunity cost attached to every public investment decision' (WPSR, 2003, p. 73). Failure to implement technology projects that mandate valuable changes is considered wasting public money. This pursued a lot of governments to assess readiness carefully before setting up journey towards the new electronic age.

From another point of view, e-readiness was needed as most societies never experienced e-government programmes before. These programmes will naturally comprise its own learning curves, so public sector leaders considered a set of identified challenges and uncertainties which formulated early e-readiness assessments. E-readiness assessment is different from feasibility studies; for example, new technologies might be used for the first time, new modes of service delivery, new roles will be proposed to be played parallel with unverified business models which need to be adopted, in addition to the expected social and economic impacts.

2.2.2 E-readiness As an Activity

We also may think of e-readiness as an activity that needs teams to tackle its tasks; it consists of a set of stages and processes that exist in any other project;

agencies need to give e-readiness projects all possible success factors due to its strategic importance.

E-readiness activities may include selecting a project team, identifying needed assessment criteria, gathering information, carrying out audits, conducting analysis, and concluding results that help in formulating e-transformation strategy.

E-readiness assessment tools vary from basic questionnaires to thorough economic and social studies; it depends on what programme owner wants to achieve exactly, and what is his allowed budget and available time frame.

Assessment objectives need to be established in order to design readiness measures; for example, assessing national level readiness may include availability of valid legal framework, or national level telecommunication infrastructure studies, while agency level readiness may include local ICT facility check, business process review, etc.

Assessment levels and activities will be comprehensively discussed in the rest of this book. Now we have to shed some light on e-readiness indices.

2.2.3 E-readiness As an Index

Many regional and global e-readiness surveys were conducted in order to classify countries in terms of e-readiness for the purpose of international benchmarking. According to Bridge Organisation, February 2005, 1506 e-readiness assessments have now been conducted; 188 countries have been assessed by at least one tool; out of the 188, 68 countries have been assessed between five to ten times by different parties, while more than sixty-nine countries have been assessed more than ten times.

These indices varied between general ICT readiness studies and more focused surveys that measure specific readiness capability; for instance e-commerce or e-government.

2.2.3.1 Generic Indicators

Digital Opportunity Index (DOI) is one well-known recent generic index; 'It has been designed as a tool for tracking progress in bridging the digital divide and the implementation of the outcomes of the World Summit on the Information Society (WSIS)' (WISR, 2007, p. 35).

First assessment results included 180 countries and first published in November 2005, then updated biannually; figure 2.1 indicates that DOI consists of three groups of indicators: opportunity, infrastructure, and utilisation.

The three tracks were purely focused on measuring the availability and usability of communication tools like phones, mobiles, broadband lines, personal computers, and the Internet users; this may reflect e-readiness to a certain extent, but not necessarily reflecting ability to build and sustain competitive edge in technology, for instance while considering mobile technology limitations in carrying out electronic transactions. Many people who use mobile phones as a substitute for regular phones may lack experience in new trends of communication, like using mobile technology in business transactions. We may have to wait for more matured mobile technologies and a new generation that is more capable of transacting online.

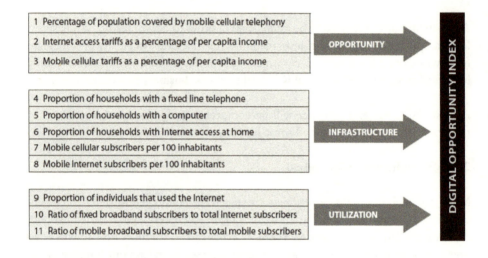

Figure 2.1: Digital Opportunity Index.
Source: World Information Society Report, 2007.

DOI is analogous to international telecom union (ITU) opportunity index (ITU-OI). 'It relies on ten indicators that help measure ICT networks, education and skills, uptake and intensity of the use of ICT by measuring the relative difference in ICT Opportunity levels among economies' (WISR, 2007, p. 16).

The advantage of DOI over ITU-OI is that DOI consider cost of service that vary widely between countries, (tariffs), while ICT-OI assess traditional ICT channels readiness in addition to literacy indicators (school enrolment).

Both indices suffer from some deficiencies; for example, world information society report argued that digital divide has many perspectives; this for sure will complicate reflecting divide in statistical analysis.

Report suggests that nation's wealth is the major factor for the divide; this was evidenced by scores that were in general differentiated according to region:

- Europe and the Americas were higher than the world average (world average is 0.40).
- Asia's average matches world average.
- Africa has an DOI score of 0.22

On opposition to the wealth theory in justifying results is Korea which ranked as number one in world digital opportunity Index (Korea Score is 0.8), yet Korea is classified as developing economy by the United Nations (WISR, 2007, p. 21).

The digital divides seem to be more than wealth; it could be part of the inherited divides between developing and developed nations. Figure 2.2 contains some interesting statistics about the key components of DOI, namely mobile phones, fixed line phones, the Internet users, and broadband lines. It shows that high income nations, who are only 15.7 per cent of the world population, form 55.7 per cent of the Internet users, using 80 per cent of fixed broadband access; this may be supporting the wealth theory to justify the gap. On the other hand we have to consider three factors. First, high income nations are technology producers which justify why it is well established in their countries; low income populations may have a list of other priorities beside technology infrastructure.

Second factor is cost of connectivity; for example, broadband connectivity cost in high income nations is much less than low income nations.

International Communication Union (ICU) justifies this by factors like:

1. Small-sized Internet markets mandates deficient economies of scale;
2. Some ddeveloping countries are using satellite access which suffers from high costs and limited bandwidth since they lack access to land or marine international lines.

Internet connectivity will cost low income nations' economies extra cost in order to settle their telecom accounts with high income nations as calls direction will flow towards the last due to their rich published digital content.

The last factor is that most low income nations suffer from undemocratic governments; they lack well-established economies and highly bureaucratic public sectors.

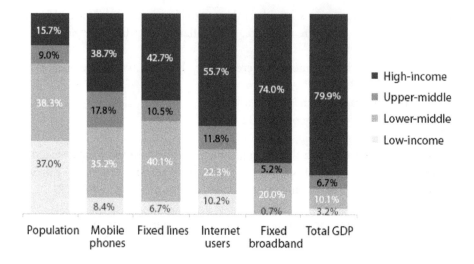

Figure: 2.2 Distribution of major ICT by income group of economies.
Source: ICT World Telecom indicators Database from WISR, 2007.
Note: Population data and ICT data are for year end 2005, GDP data for year end 2004.

2.2.3.2 Conclusion About E-Readiness Indices

Digital classifications and ranking may have convincing values for capitalists and politicians; it will provide information about contemporary trends regionally and globally. At the same time it barely has much added value at average constituent level or even give valuable information to local public sector leaders about how to draw e-government strategies.

Rather than achieving a rank, developing nations should look at technology as an economic and social development opportunity. They should adopt education and training strategies in order to grasp knowledge so as to be technology providers rather than consumers. Nurturing ICT will secure a lot of jobs for developing countries not only to cover their local needs but to plan towards making ICT industry gradually contribute to their GDPs; this will give them extra political power globally.

2.2.3.3 E-government Indicators

Parallel with generic ICT indices, many specialised e-readiness indices were developed in the last few years, for example e-government Readiness Series by United Nations Department of Economic and Social Affairs (UN-DESA), Global e-Government Rankings Series by Accenture Consulting, and the Economist Intelligence Unit e-readiness Index which measures the degree to which a society is ready for e-business opportunities (Ojo et al., 2007).

Ojo et al. argue that most indices were based on evaluating national e-government websites against stated Web maturity criteria; studies revealed that UN-DESA readiness index is the most inclusive index as it uses a structured approach of five maturity levels (emerging, enhanced, interactive, transactional, and networked); it covers human capacity development, telecommunication infrastructure, online presence, and e-participation in assessing readiness of UN member countries.

Other studied models covered fewer countries and used similar criteria with different weights of importance and maturity levels. Despite the lack of standards for e-government assessment that lead to varying conclusions on country ranking levels, nevertheless Ojo et al. statistical analysis for the three key surveys' results for the period from 2001 to 2004 indicates an increasing agreement between surveys over years.

In general, indices suffer from inaccuracy resulting from subjectivity; some indices are based on highly ready countries' scores, which makes comparison inflexible. This degrades indices value. Nevertheless, measuring and publishing e-government indices is a major driver for many politicians to continue funding and supporting technology programmes by all means to achieve better ranking and preserve their countries from being isolated by digital divide.

2.3 E-readiness Tools

The early mentioned e-readiness perspectives (requirement, activities, and indices) underline the importance of the e-readiness subject, and the possible researches it may stimulate; this book could be a small contribution.

Bridge, an independent not-for-profit organisation aiming at bridging digital divide, classifies e-readiness tools into the following:

1. Ready-to-use questionnaires which sounds to be the easiest.
2. Case studies are another approach for studying e-readiness but usually cover limited countries.
3. Independent parties' surveys like digital divide reports.

Bridge grouped e-readiness assessment tools and argued a classification of two main models: 'e-economy' and 'e-society' (Bridge.org, 2005).

E-economy readiness tools are those that assess basic ICT infrastructure to measure nation's readiness for business or economic growth. E-society oriented tools are those that focus on the ability of the overall society to benefit from ICT (Bridge. org, 2005).

'E-society' tools incorporate business growth and use of ICT as part of their larger analysis, and consider business growth necessary for society's e-readiness. 'E-economy' focused tools also include some factors of interest to the larger society, such as privacy and universal access. (Bridge.org, 2005)

More expanded e-readiness vision that incorporates both e-economy and e-society concept found in world public sector report published in 2003 which used two factors to measure in countries under study – e-readiness and e-participation.

E-readiness, which was early described, is a composite index that consists of Web Measure Index, Telecommunication Infrastructure Index, and Human Capital Index.

On the other hand, e-participation is 'the willingness, on part of the government, to provide high quality information (explicit knowledge) and effective communication tools for the specific purpose of empowering people to ably participate in consultations and decision-making, both in their capacity as consumers of public services and as citizens' (WPSR, 2003, pp. 15 and 135). This could be considered as assessment of the utilisation of ICT in democracy implementations.

As indicated earlier, e-readiness index consists of three composite indices. They are as follows:

1. Web Measure Index: It 'is a questionnaire-based quantitative index that measures the generic aptitude of governments to employ e-government as a tool to inform, interact, transact, and network. It aims at measuring e-government effectiveness in support of human development' (WPSR, 2003, p. 136).

   Same set of questions were used to assess the national portal or the official homepage of the government in addition to health, education, social welfare, labor, and finance departments' (or ministries) websites.

2. Telecommunication Infrastructure Index: It is a composite, weighted average index of well-known ICT-related infrastructure indicators which are number of personal computers, the Internet users, telephone users, mobile users, online users, and television users per thousand persons.

3. Human Capital Index: This index relies on the UNDP education index, which is a composite of the following:

   • Two third of the index is contributed from adult literacy rate.

- Other third is contributed from gross enrolment ratio including (combined primary, secondary, and tertiary education).

    'The gross enrolment ratio for a given level of education is derived by dividing the total enrolment for this level (regardless of age) by the population of the age group that should be enrolled at this level at the beginning of the academic/school year according to national regulations – definition source: ISCED, UNESCO'(UNECE, 2007).

4. E-participation Index: This resulted from the assessment of a total of twenty-one citizen informative and participatory services and facilities across six sectors which are education, health, social welfare, finance, employment, and general; the last is a free sector to be proposed by each country. Websites were assessed for democratic facilitation on three tracks: information, consultation, and decision making:

    - E-information: sites provision of information about policies; budgets; and laws, regulations and usage of online public information.
    - E-consultation: how much do websites facilitate constituents' involvement in public related discussions and information exchanging.
    - E-decision Making: how much do websites influence public sector decision making.

CHAPTER THREE

E-Readiness Model

Chapter Summary

Organisational readiness is integrated to other readiness perspectives such as global, regional and national readiness. In this chapter, I will introduce my conclusions about these mentioned perspectives in order to integrate organisational readiness with key national and regional activities in digital economy transformation programmes.

3.1 E-readiness Levels

The increased interest in e-government and e-commerce globally and the progress in digital economy facets (e-commerce, e-government, e-education, etc.) are continuously enriching e-readiness field of knowledge; we may classify e-readiness levels to be as follows:

1. Global level readiness
2. Regional level readiness
3. National level readiness
4. Industry/business sector level readiness
5. Organisation level readiness
6. Community level readiness
7. Personal level readiness

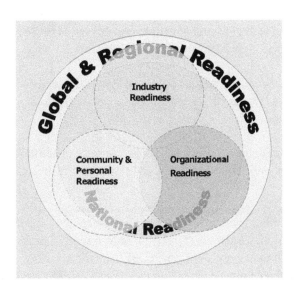

Figure 3.1: E-readiness levels.
Source: Author.

Segregating e-readiness into levels is vital for researching this topic; Figure 3.1 shows these e-readiness levels and their interdependences.

We may depict the relationships from down up; for example, in the bottom line, we found organisational readiness, intersecting with societal and business sector readiness; this means that in order to practice effective e-governments, each agency should do a set of preparations. In the meanwhile, society (including individuals and social institutions) and vertical industries have to be ready to participate effectively; this should be in full compliance with national, regional, and global readiness.

Some e-readiness criteria are common and shared between all levels of readiness; for example, it is better to recognise and enforce any protocols or standards concerning information exchanges at national, regional, and global levels; this will assist in bridging digital divide. Another example is industry level readiness criteria, for example, e-payment regulations in banking industry, must coordinate with regional standards; on the other hand, it should consider organisational readiness requirements.

This book is mainly about organisational level readiness; nevertheless, I will discuss briefly some other levels.

3.1.1 Global Level Readiness

Technology is classified as the one of the key factors for change, parallel with political, social, and economic factors, known as PEST. Countries around the world vary in developing and consuming technology; this impacts the minimum level of readiness to participate in e-government activities.

Global e-readiness could be defined as a set of factors that derive or impact nation's capacities to participate in contemporary transformation into digital economy and information society.

I formulated this definition out of many resources since the term is used to describe various meanings and extensively used politically and technically. Here are two definitions:

- Information society is 'society in which the creation, distribution, diffusion, uses, and manipulation of information is a significant economic, political, and cultural activity' (Wikipedia, 2007).
- A digital economy is 'an economy that is based on electronic goods and services produced by an electronic business and traded through electronic commerce. That is, a business with electronic production and management processes and that interacts with its partners and customers and conducts transactions through Internet and Web technologies' (Wikipedia, 2007).

Global e-readiness is extremely needed to foster climate for digital economy; for instance, telecommunications infrastructures which form the communications channels used by all countries; and as e-government mandates enormous digital exchanges via this shared infrastructure, then regulations, standardisation are needed to discipline digital relationships between nations who share this infrastructure.

One key global challenge is the identity of the Internet users which makes the Internet an unsecure place from various perspectives. Encryption and the use of digital signatures still need lots of coordination and enforcement globally; existing security tools are insufficient to secure digital traffic, which increase the demand on new security techniques. As a response, 'National Institute of Standards and Technology, USA, launched an open, blind competition to come up with a fresh algorithm for hash functions in January 2007' (WISR, 2007).

Many Internet users believe that some countries are monopolising the Internet; many think that the Internet traffic are being filtered for commercial and non-commercial reasons. The world lacks satisfactory protocols to govern digital content. This includes intellectual property and copyright laws, taxation on e-commerce sales, and security and authentication issues; these in a way or another impact readiness to e-government. In fact a set of international bodies are embarking on identifying and resolving globally common issues related to e-readiness; advancements in this direction will encourage decision makers to work hardly on their regional and local readiness to comply with global readiness. Some local and regional standards are adopted globally as best practices. For example, BS7799, which is a British security standard, was adopted by international standard organisation and became ISO-17799 security standard.

3.1.2 Regional Level Readiness

Regional level readiness is concerned with e-readiness between groups of countries based on geographical, political, or economic preferences. For example, European Union established European Network and Information Security Agency (ENISA); other recent example is Regional ICT Action Plan for Latin America and the Caribbean.

Usually neighbor nations share common resources and encounter heavy economic and societal interactions, which naturally were impacted by evolving ICT; members in regional alliances may benefit from developing common digital strategies aiming at a set of objectives such as facilitating information sharing, unifying digital protocols, developing common e-marketplaces, integrating government e-services, building electronic payment systems, and possibly managing human capital regionally by building job e-markets.

Regional e-readiness will focus on criteria needed to cater for strategic opportunities identified by sharing countries; of course, regional e-readiness will enhance other lower level readiness such as national, industry, and community levels.

3.1.3 National Level Readiness

Similar to global and regional e-readiness, each country must address a set of legislative, economic, and social limitations and catalysts which will conclude strategic initiatives that work in harmony to build and sustain national level digital competitive advantage. This seems to be a wide playing field of differentiation, since national level initiatives have more flexibility than global and regional ones; it might be hard to find regional or global partners since many countries may lack interest or feel reluctant to coordinate internationally in order to reduce scientific leakage and afraid of cat copying its own successes that would possibly decline its competitive edge.

National e-readiness is an important and integral part of the national development programmes; if e-government programmes fail to serve national strategies then it is subject to be classified as pointless programmes according to WPSR classification.

National e-readiness programmes must complement government strategies in major domains like health, education, manufacturing, tourism, trade, etc. Each country has its own mix of national resources, opportunities, and threats. This makes formulating a standard e-readiness strategy complete enough to be followed by all countries a far away dream. Another fact to consider is the high level of uncertainty surrounding digital economy structures, even those experienced by modern nations around the world; to some extent, they are still evolving experiments

One example for national readiness is countries that lack enough telecom infrastructures are working hard to liberalise their local telecom sectors. This can't be achieved without changing jurisdictions that granted telecom sectors monopolies in the past. and may require some changes in legislative and foreign investment regulations.

Countries that suffer from bureaucratic bodies need to adopt e-readiness programmes that motivate government agencies workers and leaders; motivation approaches are tightly related to cultures, so no one solution fits all nations whilst not forgetting available budgets.

To build successful e-government, many infrastructural components are involved. The following national sectors are having special readiness which accumulate national readiness and complement regional and global readiness; it is represented in figure 3.2:

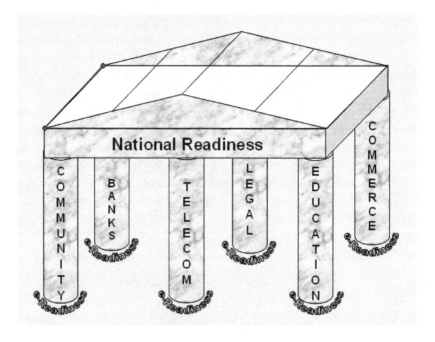

Figure 3.2: National e-government readiness.
Source: Author.

3.1.3.1 Telecom sector readiness

Telecom is at the heart of digital economy; it is a key partner in e-government success. Telecom readiness includes providing telecom solutions that suit country geographically and economically; telecom sector should involve e-government programmes requirements in its infrastructure expansions and solutions packages.

Historically, many countries used to have organised monopoly in telecom sectors which after many years hindered their abilities to cope with accelerated developments in this industry; there were many jurisdictional and political readiness complexities rather than technical limitations of telecom infrastructure.

A wave of telecom sectors privatisation was witnessed in the last 15 years which resulted in more effective and efficient services. Figure 3.3 shows the dramatically increasing number of countries that established national level regulatory agencies to strategically develop this important sector since 1990.

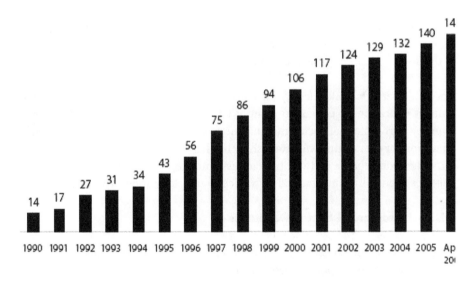

Figure 3.3: Number of economies with a national telecom regulatory agency, 1990–2007.

Source: ITU World Telecommunication Regulatory Database from WISR, 2007.

3.1.3.2 Banking Sector Readiness

Banking infrastructure is essential to cover e-payment systems. Banks led e-commerce initiatives by using electronic fund transfer systems (EFT) many years before online merchandising; 'A Federal law to allow the transfer of funds electronically was passed in the United States in 1978' (The Accounting Payable Network, 2007).

The early exploitation of ICT technology in banking services allowed banking industry an inherited e-readiness comparing with public sector. Banking sector in a given country will play an important role to support e-government programmes. Many genius e-services was based on pure utilisation of distributed banking automated teller machines (ATM), for example, paying fines and government fees from any ATM before requesting service from government agency. This formed an alternate channel for e-payment services in countries with limited Internet penetration.

Banking sector e-readiness includes technical aspects, internal business process, and legislative readiness, for example, the legality of electronic transactions and ability to customise e-payment solutions to serve e-government transactions

3.1.3.3 Academic Sector Readiness

Moving towards e-government mandates a lot of efforts from various skilled workers technically and managerially. Researchers agree that transformation to e-government consists of long-term strategic programmes; the last two facts emphasise the role of the academic sectors and their output in supporting transformation to e-government; for example, special diplomas could be arranged in this topic to help in passing enough knowledge to leaders in public sector.

Academic sector should identify all skills needed for the coming digital age, then redirect education objectives to comply with the new national digital strategies. One key part of national academic readiness is the real usage of ICT in delivering education; of course, this will establish technology usage and make a daily practice for young constituents and will help in disseminating technology and information culture which will reduce natural resistance to transformation programmes.

3.1.3.4 Commercial Sector Readiness

Commercial sector consists of various levels of businesses that have a spectrum of collaboration with public sector as a regulatory body and a customer in the same time. E-procurement is a key solution in e-government that has G2G and G2B services; this will not succeed if business sectors are not ready to participate. For example, they may lack connectivity or readiness to integrate their back-end systems with e-commerce solutions. They may feel afraid of using e-transactions and consider it unacceptable if not enough legalised by law; they may simply look at it as just redundant or unnecessary extra costs.

Early involvement of commercial sectors by identifying their e-readiness criteria, measuring it regularly and implementing recommended actions will support national e-government programmes; the last should take into consideration the for-profit nature of this sector. E-government programmes should provide opportunities rather than anything else in order to pursue these sectors to invest money in order to gain more readiness.

Commercial sector may have opportunities to partnership with public sector to build e-government components; for example, building, operating, and transferring (BOT) some infrastructural solutions needed to launch e-government services, private sector may build complete infrastructure and collect charges per transaction to return back investments over a given period of time. Such kind of partnerships may help governments which lack enough funds to support e-government initiatives; in general, developing successful private-public partnerships is a key challenge for contemporary economies.

E-government programmes should be tuned to facilitate national business sectors participation in regional and international e-commerce marketplaces; internationally, e-commerce volume is rapidly increasing and will continue to grow. E-government programmes will be wasteful if it fails to bridge e-commerce gaps between national business sectors and the rest of the world.

Various e-readiness initiatives could be arranged through business communities – for example, chamber of commerce and unions – to raise awareness of required readiness levels by each commercial subdivision.

3.1.3.5 Legislative sector readiness

Nations need to check if their legislations can support e-transformation; this includes many preventive, detective, and corrective controls. Countries vary widely in legislative issues pertaining to national e-readiness; legislations can play crucial role in protecting stakeholders' rights while developing e-commerce and e-government initiatives.

In order to build legislative readiness, two approaches of legislations need to be considered:

1. **Digital jurisdictions:** It aims at legalising electronic modes of conducting business. This includes validation of electronic forms and media, legal support for systematised electronic data exchange, digital crime related issues, etc. One good example is the United Kingdom Privacy Act of 1974, the US acts such as Electronic Communications Act 2000, Electronic Signature Regulations 2002, Electronic Commerce Regulations 2002, Personal Data Privacy and Security Act of 2005, CAN-SPAM Act of 2003, and Computer Fraud and Abuse Act 1986.
2. **Catalysts legislations**: It aims to organise and support e-government implementation; for example, Government Performance and Results

Act of 1993 (GPRA) which required all agencies to draft strategic plans by 1997 and set performance goals by 1999, Government Paperwork Elimination Act (GPEA) in 1998, and the privacy impact requirement of the E-Government Act of 2002 (Holden and Millett, 2005).

These are samples of possible acts that will regulate relationships between e-government and e-commerce stakeholders; on the other hand, it gives seriousness and commitment of political bodies to support e-government transformation.

3.1.3.6 Community readiness

Community justifies the existence of government in the first place. E-government programmes should consider involving community and assess its readiness to gradual transformation.

Using technology tools like phones, mobiles, broadband lines, and the Internet have community readiness criteria which form the other face of telecom readiness. Telecom readiness deals with availability of technology tools, while community readiness discuss ability to use these tools effectively; providing connectivity should be parallel with leveraging community utilisation of its potential benefits. People vary in their skills to utilise these tools: for example, launching e-services to a community which is not ready yet to interact with it will not end with successful implementation.

Community should be aware about new channels benefits. It should also feel satisfied about security issues; some e-government programmes aim at enforcing constituents' satisfaction and trust of its government under the evolving concept of e-democracy. E-democracy is 'the utilization of electronic communications technologies, such as the Internet, in enhancing democratic processes within a democratic republic or representative democracy' (Wikipedia, 2007).

Investing in technology should be parallel with demand for technology in order to achieve best economic value for governmental expenditure. We already discussed e-government programmes opportunity cost which should be measured against other initiatives that seek nation's prosperity.

One final word is that community level readiness contains the early mentioned personal readiness; personal readiness may vary within community according to the needs and abilities; there are many possible readiness segmentations within community based on age, sex, culture, education, profession, and so; this highlights that community readiness assessment programmes must analyse national demographical distribution before concluding initiatives to rectify gaps in community readiness in preparation for transformation to e-government.

Part Two

Organisational E-Readiness

CHAPTER FOUR

E-readiness Model

Chapter Summary

In this chapter, I will conclude an organisational e-readiness model that could be followed by scholars and public sector planners in order to assess and audit organisations' abilities in a structured way; this includes both public sector agencies as well as private sectors.

As organisational readiness is part of regional and global readiness, I will introduce my conclusions about global, regional, and national e-readiness for more in-depth analysis and to integrate organisational readiness with key national and regional activities in digital economy transformation programmes.

Proposed organisational model consists of five key categories of criteria, which are strategy readiness, business process readiness, technology, IT security, and finally and importantly, ability for organisational change.

4.1 Introduction

E-GOVERNMENT initiatives are considered a continuation to public sector modernisation efforts, according to many resources, for example, Ebrahim and Irani (2005) and Gascó (2007). Nations which started such modernisation programmes early in the sixties and seventies of the last century will for sure enjoy more readiness to implement e-government initiatives.

Modernisation programmes were mainly aimed at enhancing operating environment in public sector. These programmes took various approaches, for example, adopting total quality management (TQM) concepts, ISO compliancy programmes, business process reengineering (BPR), in addition to office automation and strategic management initiatives.

Modernisation programmes in all shapes formed a challenge for public sector leaders exactly as current e-government programmes. It used to be faced by human resistance, which to a certain extent is a natural response. Successfully managing expected change is a key success factor that is shared by all modernisation endeavors.

There are various e-government readiness criteria at the organisation level, which will be investigated and discussed in the coming sections; it forms the body of this book.

Before discussing organisation level readiness, we have to realise two important things: first, understand the components of a standard e-readiness model, and second, to review a sample e-government model. Basically, we have to agree that organisational readiness need to be measured against a stated or agreed upon e-government model. This is justified by the following:

1. The need for agencies to identify their specific possible role in the national or regional e-government programme according to programme strategic objectives and existing stage of implementation; this will lead to a set of straightforward objectives that need to be met at the organisation level.

    For example, during Web presence stage of e-government, the agency that is responsible for education (say ministry of education) has certain requirements to prepare for effective participation, while keeping eyes on the next stages which will require extra readiness, for instance, building infrastructure for e-education.

2. 'Bitability'[1] of core strategic services versus supportive administrative processes is widely varying between agencies; each organisation has to develop its own strategy for transformation parallel with other agencies. This emphasises the importance of national level e-government model that has its specific objectives and e-readiness programmes.

3. Some agencies introduce services that are shared with other parties. E-readiness for integrated services needs to be discussed with related

---

[1]   See Section 1.1 e-government definition.

parties, for example, central government, other agencies, private sector organisations, and specialised sectors like banking and telecom. National e-government model is the umbrella which will secure a minimum level of coordination.

For a sample of e-government model, readers are advised to review appendix I. It contains description of business and technical architectures that need to be developed at the national level since what an e-government programme wants to achieve at a given stage will determine organisational readiness programme that firm should pursue while taking into consideration available budget.

In addition to that, organisational readiness must comply with global and regional readiness; it also should comply with the other six pillars of national readiness as the organisation is not isolated from these sectors.

Before introducing the proposed organisational e-readiness model, which is supposed to have specific auditable and measurable criteria, I would like to discuss possible components of a generic readiness model; this will help the reader integrate transformation objectives with the auditable e-readiness model components and how we can deliver readiness assessment as a practical project.

4.2 E-readiness Model Components

At each e-readiness level, there are a set of readiness criteria that have various weights of importance according to e-government's maturity stage (phase). Readiness criteria are based on barriers, limitations, as well as potential opportunities.

E-readiness model components are as follows:

1. **Criteria**: based on clear strategic objectives.
2. **Methods**: Assessment methods of measurement.
3. **Audit**: Revisions and Results.
4. **Initiatives**: Activities to be considered in order to bridge gaps.
5. **Monitoring**: Follow up system to secure readiness continuity.

4.2.1 Criteria

As indicated in figure 4.1, each nation has its own existing limitations and barriers, but is looking ambitiously to a desired situation in the future that is full of opportunities, though having its own uncertainties. E-readiness is the structured tool that will ease transformation through specific initiatives to develop infrastructure, business process, and human abilities needed for the desired situation.

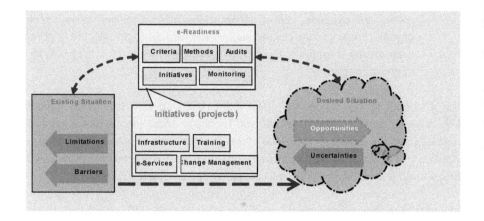

Figure 4.1: Using e-readiness to facilitate organisational transformation.
Source: Author.

The drawing also indicates that organisations have to identify the characteristics of the desired situation in order not to make e-government a vague target. With the existence of uncertainties which have been reduced after years of e-government experiments, readiness programmes may need to stage desired situation targets in order to gain more control over e-government long-term programmes. This will directly influence what criteria needs to be introduced in each stage as a minimum requirement without overwhelming organisations with unnecessary burdens.

4.2.2 Assessment Methods

When assessment criteria is identified, methods for testing and grading schemes need to be developed; in fact, some criteria may be hard to quantify, or may be subject to bias while collecting information. This emphasises the importance of following professional audit methods to seek accurate results. Defining assessment methods will standardise assessment and reduce bias and errors during audit exercises. It will help the team measure same criterion in many organisation and benchmark results.

Some criteria pertaining to agency capabilities may use a common maturity assessment approach adopted from CMMI and COBIT Governance Models; it consists of six levels as follows:

1. **Does not exist**: no clear evidence that specific readiness factor has been practiced or even realised.
2. **Add hoc**: there were rare cases where specific readiness factor has been used on casual bases.

3. **Repeated**: readiness factor is known and preferred but not enforced officially, yet it is supported individually.
4. **Defined**: criterion is officially part of organisation management system; it is documented and standardised.
5. **Managed**: criterion is monitored and measured; it is part of periodic assessment mechanism in addition to clearly assigned responsibility and ownership.
6. **Optimised**: best practices pertaining to a specific criterion are facilitated and every opportunity for improvement is efficiently used.

Figure 4.2 represents these maturity ladder levels:

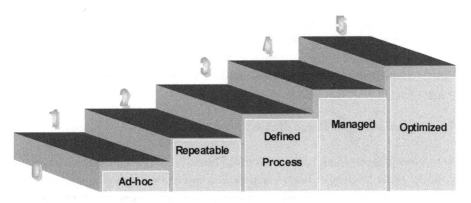

Figure: 4.2: Maturity model ladder.
Source: **Raj, R.Vittal, 2004, IT Governance strategies for continuous process improvement, Asia CACS conference, Dubai, December, 2004.**

4.2.3 Audit

As you see, the proposed model segregated criteria assessment methods from audits. Each criterion will have one assessment method or more, then audit schemes need to be identified to measure and re-measure readiness criterion. Audit standards adopted from other professions (for instance, financial, ICT, and ISO audit) could be followed to secure a high level of accuracy in data gathering; these standards include audit code of conduct, planning and execution, sampling techniques, and reporting.

4.2.4 Initiatives

Initiatives are activities that need to be done in order to bridge the gap. It may vary from simple tasks to multimillion dollar infrastructural projects. Initiatives are key recommendations concluded out of e-readiness assessment. It might be directed to federal government in order to take actions on county or national levels; a good example is jurisdictional related issues. On the other hand, initiatives might be directed to a specific organisation in order to consider some actions pertaining to certain e-readiness criteria, for example, lack of security devices (say, a firewall), or automation of strategic business processes.

Initiatives must comply with readiness criteria as well as e-government programme objectives; on the other hand, many initiatives need funding in order to be accomplished, so they need to be reasonably justified.

4.2.5 Monitoring

Assessment is not a one-time activity that serves specific result, unless agency ceased e-government programme! So it need to continuously assess its readiness to the next stage of implementation. E-readiness assessment is the first step in e-government transformation and will continue to be used to assess advancements in gap filling at all levels.

4.3 Organisational E-readiness

Now we will be returning back to our initial question: What agencies' leaders need to do in order to prepare to participate in e-government programmes? And as we emphasised in earlier chapters on the importance of leadership in charging and empowering staff to accept and participate in positive change. Such healthy organisations that own the ability to successfully accept changes are known as learning organisations.

Learning organizations continuously learns through its members individually and collectively to create a sustainable competitive advantage by effectively managing internally and externally generated change. (Sudharatna and Li, 2007)

Major traits of learning organisations are around human related factors, as argued by Sudharatna and Li. These characteristics could be grouped in the following:

1. Cultural values
2. Leadership
3. Commitment and empowerment
4. Communication and knowledge transfer
5. Employee characteristics and performance upgrading

Understanding 'learning organisation' concepts will help us in building organisation level e-readiness model. In fact, there is so much debate on organisational e-readiness as the level of readiness in public sector agencies will vary according to possible participation in e-government programmes. This made it hard to depend on one model that leverages agencies into required readiness.

Previous facts indicate that building a standard e-readiness model that serve at organisation level is so hard yet never impossible. From the reviewed literature and practical experience, I concluded the following organisation e-readiness tracks:

1. Strategy readiness
2. Business readiness
3. Technology readiness
4. Culture readiness (ability to change)
5. ICT Security readiness

These intersected and tightly related tracks outline key pillars for any ICT based transformation. In simple words, agency needs clear strategic direction, which will support reformulation of strategy derived business processes to be enabled using technology by its wide means. If these three factors are ready, organisation needs change supportive environment like managed risks and sincere leadership in order to carry it out successfully.

Due to the criticality of information security, it is receiving increasing concerns from stakeholders and has already been discussed as one of the barriers for e-government transformation. Security has been assigned a separate readiness track as it has various perspectives (strategic, business, and technical).

Each organisational readiness track includes a lot of sub-criteria that we will discuss in the following sections.

CHAPTER FIVE

Strategy Readiness

Chapter Summary

The first organisational readiness group of criteria is the strategy readiness. Without clear strategy, firms will go nowhere. Strategic management includes planning and performing in a strategic way. Readiness model suggests five sub-criteria, namely strategic planning, organisational structure, functions and services, performance management, and informational model.

5.1 Introduction

STRATEGIC management and transformational leadership style are two key factors that contribute to the success of e-government initiatives (Wenbo, 2002); this is true on national level as well as organisational level. Strategic management is the recommended style of management that incorporates performance management in the operational level to help implementing strategic plans.

E-government initiatives must promote strategic planning and management as part of the readiness in order to effectively manage the investments in technology and human resources mandated by the e-government programmes; for example, in the absence of strategic management at agency level, how agency's staff will be able to assess the effectiveness and performance of launched e-services, or how they will prioritise key business processes that directly affect agency strategy and delay those who do not directly support agency strategy.

'Managers who operate from a strategic management perspective first and foremost create public value' (Berry, 2007), while 'public agencies with considerable goal ambiguity tend to have a difficult time strategising and implementing management innovations' (Berry et al., 1997). Strategy readiness assessment contains two major areas: strategic planning and strategic management. Strategy assessment could be accomplished by assessing the following four parts:

1. Strategic Planning
2. Organisational structure
3. Functions and services
4. Performance management
5. Informational Model

The following sections will discuss each of the strategy readiness criterions.

5.2 Strategic Planning

Strategy readiness could be defined as the minimum level of strategy awareness and practices in planning and management that assure protecting investments in e-government initiative. Clearly identified and well-communicated strategic direction including vision, mission, and strategic objectives will cover strategic planning stage; if seconded with performance management system to gauge strategy implementation, then the agency will assure a high level of strategy readiness.

Strategic planning was cited as the most widely implemented reform of this group, lending credence to the assertion that strategic planning is both widely used and becoming more integrated into broader management reform efforts. (Berry, 2007)

Managers in agencies with effective strategic planning systems felt that strategic planning made their agency more flexible in dealing with external and internal changes than did managers in agencies without solid strategic planning systems. (Huang, 1997, from Berry, 2007)

5.3 Strategic Management

The other part of strategy readiness is the management part. Many organisations succeed in strategic planning but fail in implementation; I think this part is represented and could be assessed using four interrelated components. These are as follows:

1. Organisational Structure
2. Functions and services
3. Performance management
4. Informational model

Each of the above is vital for the strategy level readiness in any firm. Organisational structure must support the strategic objectives of the organisation and complies with its services, while performance management is needed to measure strategy effectiveness in terms of its structure and services. Informational model represents the strategic planning for IT in order to assure effective and economical use of ICT resources.

5.3.1 Organisational Structure

'Organisational structure is the way in which the interrelated groups of an organisation are constructed. The main concerns are effective communication and coordination' (Wikipedia, 2007). It includes responsibilities, authorities, and relationships between stakeholders inside and outside the organisation. Ineffective organisational structure means limited capabilities, bottlenecks, non-streamlined processes, and low or extreme utilisation of resources.

Organisational structure assessment may include many criteria, starting from the availability of documented and updated organisation structure. Documentation need to be communicated and recognised by stakeholders; it should cover all strategic departments and activities, identify relationships, and authorities. Organisational structure is not one picture that shows departments in a tree-like diagram. It is a living document that reflects agency resources and services seconded with a mechanism to modify or enhance the structure when needed. Human resources jobs titles, responsibilities, and accountability inside organisation should also be integrated to organisational structure.

Figure 5.1 represents the above-mentioned readiness criteria pertaining to organisational structure:

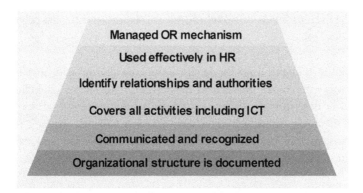

Figure 5.1: Organisation structure readiness levels.
Source: Author.

Organisational structure assessment should also include ICT function positioning to assess its level of empowerment to contribute in strategic planning and execution; this will be discussed in the informational vision and technical readiness. Recently, ICT governance models recommends shared committee between ICT, top management and business managers to lead ICT in organisations; for example, COBIT governance framework provided many best practices in organising ICT function which will help in sustaining and extending ICT value within organisations.

In order to audit organisation structure readiness, we need to assess according to the mentioned gradual maturity model; first we check for its existence by just simply asking about its availability, then we need to check latest update date – if it is matching current practices in daily work. Or if there were many modifications in business level strategies without updating organisational structure, or possibly new departments or sections were created, eliminated, or encountered changes in responsibilities without updating organisational structure.

For each level of maturity, we need to recommend an initiative to promote to next level, for example, for agencies who have a structure which is ineffectively integrated to human resources, we advise management to embark on a new project to validate or then align it with human resources.

5.3.2 Functions and Services

Functions and services refer to what an organisation is exactly doing to achieve its objectives. Away from normal administrative and housekeeping activities, what are agency departments doing and what services and products they introduce to various levels of stakeholders, for example, citizens, private sector, other agencies, etc.

We may classify activities done by departments into internal and external services. Internal services are those introduced to internal beneficiaries (stakeholders), for instance, other departments within organisation, while external services are those introduced to parties outside it. This classification will help agency to draw its e-services strategy by prioritising strategic services internally and externally in order to automate and enable using ICT.

E-readiness assessment audit should verify if functions and services are reasonably integrated to organisation's strategy. Mapping services and strategic objectives is a healthy exercise and will help organisation avoid reproducing its bureaucracy while transforming to e-government.

Readiness criteria include clearly defined and strategically mapped business processes (internal and external), assigned responsibilities (process ownership), process optimisation, and level of automation and integration with incentive system.

5.3.3 Performance Management

Performance management is 'a systematic, integrated management approach that links enterprise strategy to core processes and activities. By providing planning, budgeting, analysis and reporting capabilities; performance management allows the business to be "run by the numbers" and measurements to drive management decisions' (Wikipedia, 2007).

The ability to measure and manage performance is very essential to organisational transformation; hence it's a biller in our e-readiness model. Performance management is compactly integrated to strategic management. 'Strategic planning can help in managing change through linking agency strategies with performance measures' (Berry, 2007).

Performance management requires the implied capability of performance measurement, as 'Monitoring progress made towards achieving program goals requires systematic measurement. ICT has facilitated the processing of unprecedented amounts of program data more efficiently than ever before' (Newcomer, 2007).

Targeting specific performance levels requires identification of the existing levels. Berry argued that 'some agencies gather data by regions and use their best performing region as their target performance; other agencies may set incremental percentage increases in performance based on some trend data from past performance or expectations based on new technology or process improvement. Without prior data on program outputs and outcomes, setting targets is at best an imprecise science' (Berry, 2007).

Agencies that lack performance management capability may fail to manage the performance of reformed business processes, for example, launching e-services over the Web.

Assessment of performance management will follow generic maturity model (see section 4.2.2) to help audit team rank readiness in a unified systematic way.

5.3.4 Informational Model

Informational model is 'a high-level roadmap containing software, hardware, and other information technology requirements for healthy and securely managed information systems' (HSE-MIS, 2001).

Informational model is part of organisation strategy. It became essential due to the increased dependency of business process on ICT. An organisation should consider all available ICT potential facilitation while embarking on building its strategy. ICT open a lot of opportunities for organisations. At the same time technical factors are key factors to be assessed while conducting PEST and SWOT analysis.

Building agency informational model parallel with business strategy development will add value to the strategic planning for e-transformation. Delaying information model to later steps after building the business model may bring one key threat of being unable to change or customise business model to expand or boost ICT utilisation. It also may increase the chance that agency reproduce its existing status queue in an electronic shape, exactly as what was experienced in early automation experiments when ICT value hindered by mapping existing manual processes into screens and reports.

These valid points emphasise again the importance of ICT function positioning in organisation; early described ICT strategic involvement in strategy building mandate high empowerment for ICT team in order to help building up effective business strategy.

Information analysis exercises will define data requirements, which will be used to identify possible information architectures, and select one optimum informational model. Developed informational model usually includes data architecture and standards, information security, reporting management, and the information necessary to support the processes.

Informational model also includes building technical model to serve business model; technical model defines ICT services channels, equipments, and resources parallel with operating requirements.

Assessment includes validation of data requirements definition, in-house versus outsourcing needed ICT services, centralised and distributed data processing requirements, business continuity strategy including possible disaster recovery options and technological directions pertaining to software, hardware, databases, networking, and not forgetting human resources.

Figure 5.2 summarises strategy e-readiness criteria.

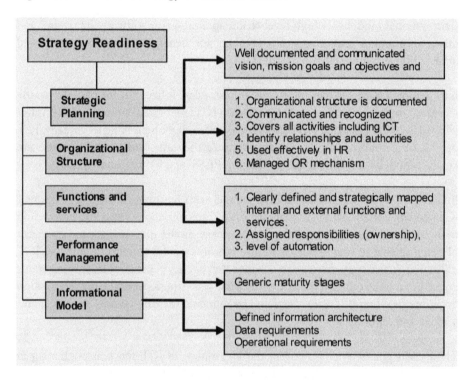

Figure 5.2: Strategy e-readiness criteria.
Source: Author.

CHAPTER SIX

Business Process Readiness

Chapter Summary

The second biller in organisational e-readiness model is the business process readiness criteria. In this chapter, I will discuss how we can assess business process readiness by integrating key factors that affect business process maturity and may form a source of threats to the process transformation at micro level or create strategy divergence while transforming traditional processes into e-services.

I am proposing four criteria to assess business process readiness. These are as follows:

- Documentation,
- Effectiveness,
- Performance evaluation, and
- Automation

6.1 Introduction

A business process is a 'collection of activities that takes one or more kinds of input and creates an output that is of value to the customer' (Credit Research Foundation, 2007), or 'business process is a recipe for achieving a commercial result. Each business process has inputs, method and outputs. The inputs are a pre-requisite that must be in place before the method can be put into practice. When the method is applied to the inputs then certain outputs will be created' (Wikipedia, 2007).

As explained earlier in strategy readiness, functions and services are considered an integral part of agency strategy. Functions or services are considered the 'what' part, where the business processes represents the 'how' part.

Assuming valid functions and services, agency managers need to know if their business processes are ready to serve in the electronic age or not; what enhancements opportunities are there to leverage organisational e-readiness in this perspective; I propose four criteria to assess business processes e-readiness:

1. Documentation
2. Effectiveness
3. Performance Evaluation
4. Automation

The following sections contain a description for each of the above factors.

6.2 Business Process Documentation

I believe that business processes documentation (BPD) is a very basic requirement and considered the first step in any organisational development efforts; it is a prerequisite to other business processes readiness. Without documentation there will be no consensus on what staff has to do and how; roles and responsibilities cannot be built for undocumented processes.

Business processes in public sectors are usually built on accumulative official documents pertaining to agency, like initiation and declaration document, with a series of upgrading and modification decrees; these forms agency business process framework and initial documentation. Further detailing levels of business processes documentation is varying from agency to another. Some agencies have detailed documentation to all business processes, roles and responsibilities, controls, and exception handling.

Modernisation initiatives like implementing ISO quality framework, and automation in agencies were good drivers to process documentation as it formed a basic requirement; these initiatives improved business process e-readiness in general.

In order to assess business process documentation, we need to measure and evaluate the following criteria:

1. Availability of a business process committee
2. Availability of updated documentation for all strategic processes
3. Accessibility of documentation
4. Availability of Electronic workflow systems
5. Integration of BPD to human resources roles and responsibilities.
6. Integration of BPD to automated systems.

While auditing e-readiness, auditor should reasonably inspect and evidence these mentioned criteria; for example, auditor may start asking about business process committee. Did the organisation form any team or committee who will be responsible for the business processes? If such a team is available, then he need to assess its effectiveness by validating its formation charter, its level of formality, empowerment, work plans, roles and responsibilities, and evidenced follow-up mechanisms for its activities.

Auditor then can inspect published documentation, check if it is sound and current, and if agency's staff knows about it, do they have access to it. In fact modern workflow systems facilitated documentation and sharing of business processes information, in addition to integration with back-end systems and applications' access rights systems, which is based on staff's roles and responsibilities.

Organisations that complete the above-mentioned criteria had covered one e-transformation requirement, and will have higher opportunity to successfully transform their conventional service channels into electronic means by reengineering 'bitable' processes and digitally enable them in collaboration with related stakeholders.

6.3 Business Process Effectiveness

No doubt that documentation covers the realisation part of business processes; effectiveness is about delivering value to stakeholders economically with best quality in terms of product or service, time and cost. The following criteria could be used to assess business processes effectiveness:

1. Clarity of process drivers, initiators, triggers, and inputs
2. Clarity of process roles and responsibilities in various stages
3. Clarity of process exceptions and predefined handlings
4. Clarity of process controls and related objectives
5. Clarity of process outputs in various stages
6. Mechanisms to monitor adherence to process qualities
7. Level of support available at each stage

Staff needs to know when and where a given process starts; some services are initiated by stakeholders, for example, submission of service request. Others are initiated periodically, like tax reminders. Staff also needs to know who do what, especially for processes which are shared between departments and other external parties (e.g. other agencies, federal government). Staffs needs to understand various controls in process and why these controls are established, situations when it could be bypassed, and expected deliverables at various stages.

These seven criteria need to be assessed for key strategic processes or services using a grading scheme in order to identify possible gaps, in addition to special initiatives that could be recommended to rectify the gap.

There is another effectiveness perspective that is about the effectiveness of the whole process to achieve its stated strategic objectives; this is measured in the next business process performance evaluation criteria.

6.4 Business Process Performance

Measuring business process performance (BPP) is very essential in readiness criteria. BPP aims mainly at business process optimisation and stakeholders' satisfaction. BPP will help agency monitor process effectiveness and find reasons and ways for enhancement. Performance management ability discussed at strategy level is closely integrated to BPP; consolidated BPP outcomes are valuable inputs to strategy performance.

Performance could be measured at process steps (tasks) level, or at participant's levels in order to quantify process performance. I think agencies that have performance management in place are more ready to transform to e-government; in fact e-government might be a natural result of progressive performance enhancement activities.

E-readiness audit team may consider the common maturity scale (see Section 4.2.2) in assessing business process performance in order to conclude BPP level.

6.5 Business Process Automation

Automation is about obtaining, storing, sharing, and exchanging electronic information that pertains to business processes. In this part of business process readiness, agency needs to consider two key criteria:

1. Level of automation of various processes tasks and steps.
2. Ability to integrate and exchange digital information with other stakeholders.

Level of automation indicators may include percentage of fully automated processes. Usually, back-end systems are used to automate business processes while maintaining quality information principles; for example, information sharing and exchanging between participants in process tasks should consider minimal redundancy in information items. Back-end systems (applications) readiness will be discussed later in technology readiness.

Beside automation, the ability to provide digital information includes extra level of readiness, including sharing and transforming digital content in real time; for example, some agencies built perfect back-end systems that run in a closed operating environment that have no provision for any online integration. This will mandate developing new back-end systems that cater for this capability.

In automation, we will stop at this two criteria pertaining to automation as technology readiness track will include many other capabilities.

Figure 6.1 summarises the business process e-readiness criteria:

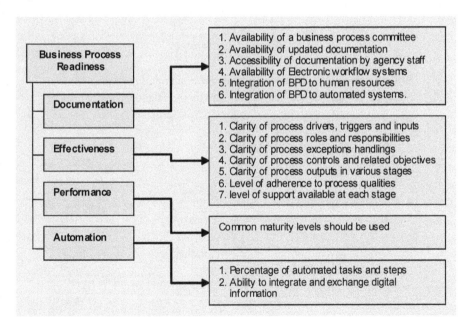

Figure 6.1: Business process e-readiness criteria.
Source: Author.

CHAPTER SEVEN

Information Technology Readiness

Chapter Summary

Information technology readiness in general includes all resources required to build, operate, and maintain technical e-transformation requirements. It contains five major components:

1. Infrastructures
2. Databases
3. Applications
4. ICT management
5. Technical skills

Each of the above contains sophisticated sub-criteria that will be discussed in this chapter.

7.1 Introduction

IN general, this includes all resources required to build, operate and maintain technical e-government requirements. This criteria contains four major components:

1. Infrastructure (capacity and scalability)
2. Databases management system

3. Applications
4. ICT management
5. Technical skills

In the following sections, I will discuss each of the above-mentioned technical readiness criteria.

7.2 Infrastructure

Infrastructure consists of the necessary physical equipment (servers, power supply, network devices, cabling, etc.); we may classify these into three major groups:

1. **Hardware**: including all devices needed to provide electronic services. Hardware e-readiness includes availability and scalability matters.
2. **Communication Network**: including local area network (LAN), wide area network (WAN), and other wireless and virtual communication apparatus. From implementation perspectives, new classification for network is currently used that includes three levels (Intranet, Internet, and Extranet).
3. **ICT Facility**: data center core room should be equipped with required environmental and physical security; this includes a suitable place to host ICT infrastructures. It needs to be reasonably secured from environmental and physical risks like fire alarms, redundant electricity sources, uninterrupted power supply (UPS), air conditioning, etc.

Needed equipments will vary according to informational architecture adopted; however, the audit team need to inspect agency infrastructure scalability based on usage expectations of data processing and network traffic, especially when offering Web enabled services to a wide range of users; capacity management is one key part of ICT management responsibilities. It is done in full coordination with operating team by monitoring average and seasonal usage.

Any identified gaps in this domain need to be rectified by an initiative; actually, there are many widely accepted quality criteria pertaining to data centers. It should be followed in order to assure higher availability for information equipments.

7.3 Databases

Conducting business online is a key facet of digital age, so an organisation will gain more readiness when it owns more strategic data in digital formats. Database readiness includes owning accumulated cleansed current and historical data in normalised databases that pertains to business and operations; this includes unique data items, systematic encoding, and updated data dictionary.

Some agencies own huge historical digital records, but they are doubtful to enable it for online inquiries as it is not verified and may contain redundant records. Some organisations realised the importance of historical records and build digital data warehouses to facilitate statistical analysis; of course, this will enhance organisational performance. Such initiatives resulted in cleansed and well-structured historical information.

Database readiness include ability to share and transfer data to Web content; some technical reasons may form a barrier for Web enabling like lack of conversion protocols for obsolete digital formats, national language problems, online database connectivity (ODBC) throughout, and Web browser version discrepancies. Such limitations could be solved by replicating data in modern databases that support Web integration, yet this may not provide 100 per cent online services as data need to be migrated periodically to reflect updates in both sides.

Database readiness also include availability countermeasures starting with effective database administration, utilisation of parallel replication of database management systems (DBMS), and providing enough licensing of concurrent users of DBMS. As the agency expands its online services, database security issues like integrity and availability became more crucial. Database readiness include data retention policies and backup systems as part of agency's comprehensive business continuity plans. This will be discussed in the security track of e-readiness.

7.4 Application

Most resources define application software as computer programmes that are used to perform specific data processing for users. Waves of business automation since the sixties of the last century[2] resulted in a lot of legacy systems that successfully automated various business aspects of public sector. In most cases, automation replicated existing manual business processes whilst embedding lot of controls in automated processes, which were impossible to embed in pure manual system. The contemporary Internet phenomenon opened doors for radical changes in business process and stakeholders' interrelationships.

Applications readiness depends on nationally adopted e-government model and the specific role of the agency; nevertheless, some general readiness criteria should

---

[2]   By the year 1962, there were over 10,000 business computers in Western Europe, and over 40,000 in the United States. In just one year, those numbers doubled. *Source:* Oracle Education Foundation (www.thinkquest.org).

be inspected at least for applications that serve strategic functions and services. It includes four key criteria:

1. Application functional maturity
2. Application maintainability
3. Application integration ability
4. Application security

7.4.1 Application Functional Maturity

Functional maturity refers to the level of automation or electronic processing coverage of application to the specific service or function that will be transformed into new means of digital based service; for example if the service is to issue tax clearance paper, this service may start by manual submission of clearance request by the constituent, then clerk will feed this in the computer application directly after receiving it, computer system will register this request, do some processing, and then either accept and print a clearance paper, or reject if the applicant has some dues. Paper may need to be signed and stamped from the manager for authenticity before it is delivered to the applicant. This process cycle may be converted into e-services in many ways, in the early stages of e-government. Service requests could be filled online as G2C service, then clearance or apology will be mailed to applicant, bearing in mind that service conventional channel is still active. In later stages of e-government transformation, this piece of information will be converted into G2G services between concerned agencies as the applicant wanted this paper simply to present it to another agency.

Application software readiness in this illustration is firstly to continue accepting manual services, secondly being able to segregate online services from manual ones. This may be achieved by having a tag or separate serial number for online transactions; online services may be assigned to a separate user in the system. Thirdly and finally application should be ready to report the status of online processed requests. When building the G2G services, same database will be accessed by newly developed application to respond to online requests received from various agencies; same application could be modified or expanded to cater for this new facilitation in business process.

We may conclude that application readiness will assess the maturity of existing applications to support the intended staged transformation.

7.4.2 Application Maintainability

From the previous example we can conclude that application maintainability is a valid readiness criterion. Applications usually under continuous development and enhancement to reflect required changes in business logic and optimise data processing.

Assessment of maintainability includes the availability of the following:

1. Application documentation.
2. Experienced resources.
3. License agreement that allow modification.
4. Effective application development and change management life cycle.

7.4.3 Application Integration Ability

Application software is running (functioning) in a platform of hardware and operating systems. Passing or extracting any data out of this harmony may be so simple if integration capability is built in this harmony; it might be a challenge if not. Currently, many parties are developing middleware software tools that facilitate integration; again integration is a valid application readiness criterion. Agencies have to decide on building new applications or integrating legacy systems using middleware tools. Aim is to effectively integrate systems in real time to exchange information in both directions to support transformation.

7.4.4 Application Security

Application security may include a set of factors, for example, access rights, input validation, and audit logs of users' activities. Without a minimum level of security, application may fail to support transformation. Applications that have limited controls in user access rights or lack audit logs to trace transaction need to be upgraded or replaced before integrating with e-services. Assessment includes benchmarking agency against known application security best practices.

7.5 ICT Management

E-government requires increased dependency on ICT that necessitate more matured management to provide and sustain healthy ICT services. Starting from strategy readiness, we articulated the importance of leveraging ICT function to participate effectively in strategy formulation and be closely involved with business process reengineering. ICT management should play a balanced role in leading e-government transformation.

ICT management readiness includes all accepted best practices argued by governance models such as COBIT and ITIL. Major ICT management readiness includes the following key criteria:

1. Organisation structure
2. ICT processes readiness

7.5.1 Organisation Structure

Organising ICT function (departments) was always challenging; it could be best serviced by team work due to the nature of technology. No typical organisational structure (OR) could be recommended as agencies will vary in size, level of automation, and expected role in e-government model.

In addition to what previously mentioned in strategy readiness about ICT function positioning in agency's organisational structure, in technical readiness, we will assess internal ICT function organisational structure to measure if it is satisfactory to support transformation. We need to assess if sub-functions suit expected role. In fact this seems to be a subjective matter. For example, some agencies outsource certain functions while others have their own teams; this will affect OR. Audit team also needs to verify if OR support segregation of duties according to recommended governance models; for example, development team is separate from production database administration team.

Organisational structure should contain independent quality assurance role, user support role for instance help desk, distributed responsibilities to avoid bottlenecks; it should also include business roles side by side to pure technical roles. It should facilitate team work and resource substitution between various sub-functions.

ICT organisational structure should also follow organisation structure maturity levels mentioned early in strategy readiness (see figure 5.1).

7.5.2 ICT Processes Readiness

ICT function or department in agency should develop fully documented policies and procedures to be followed in various technical and managerial aspects. All IT processes need to be identified and documented. It need to be assigned to resources officially in documented job description in order to assign responsibility and establish accountability; this is considered basic requirement in ICT management best practices.

Standard operating procedures cover daily operating tasks like start up, shut down, log records inspection, incident response management, configuration management, system development lifecycle, change management, periodic facility maintenance (AC, electricity, alarm system, etc.), access controls review, and so on.

ICT function should develop and enforce project management best practices, in addition to service level agreement management. Part of ICT processes are those related to human resources management. We feel that part of ICT management readiness is to control human resources risks by adopting policies for hiring, terminating, developing, training, and motivating ICT team. These policies should be communicated and integrated with human resources policies and procedures in order to reduce the impact of various human resources threats.

7.5.3 Technical Skills

There are various skills and talents needed in order to gain and sustain readiness to support electronic government operations. Recently, many organisations require much less capabilities and skills than what is required to provide twenty-four-hour online services. This raises the importance of nurturing and developing special skills that are needed more than any time before.

Required skills are many and will vary according to the following factors:

- Level of maturity of agency's ICT function.
- Agency's e-government strategic plan.
- The role of outsourcing versus in-house team members.
- Available options for agency to gain new skills and capabilities.

For example, agencies that lack suitable back-end systems may need to build their strategic applications, first, taking into consideration new business processes, or agencies with no previous Web development experiences may need to build or outsource Web development skills such as hosting, portal programming, and ability to diagnose and solve data integration problems. Another example is agencies with limited budgets to hire new team members may develop existing staff capabilities to cater for the required skills.

Regardless of readiness level, agencies have to verify that their ICT functions own the following skills:

- Capable operations staff for systems and networks
- Capable database administration

- Programming and software development methodologies
- Business analysis and processes reengineering
- Software engineering and integration
- Security specialist
- ICT quality specialist
- Project management skills

These in general are the required skills, and detailed specialty will be based on existing and planned technical informational environment. Figure 7.1 summarises technology readiness criteria.

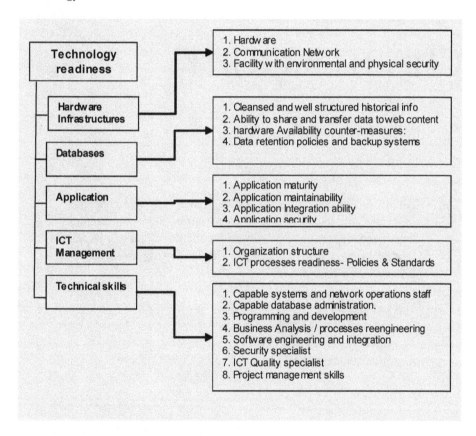

Figure 7.1: Technology e-readiness criteria.
Source: Author.

CHAPTER EIGHT

Ability to Change Readiness

Chapter Summary

Ability to change the existing status queue is a real challenge, especially in public sector due to established bureaucracy. Organisations need to be ready to handle these kinds of human related issues. I have characterised the following key readiness criteria in this regard:

1. Leadership
2. Human resource alignment
3. Effective communication
4. Risk Management

8.1 Introduction

From the early mentioned information about organisational e-readiness, we realised that e-transformation has a lot of preparations that start with strategic readiness in order to make sure that we are doing the right activities, and resources are aligned in a way that serves this direction. And we found that technical readiness and business process readiness assessment will make sure that we are doing it right and will result a beneficial transformation.

Ability to change the existing status quo is a real challenge, especially in public sector due to established bureaucracy. In simple words, what will make such change happen? First of all, is it really welcomed by stakeholders? I think stakeholders may have different point of views and various levels of impacts on the transformation. For example, some managers may stop transformation programme due to many reasons as far as he or she owns the power to; meanwhile constituents would welcome such transformation. Political parties may argue about the feasibility of investing tax payers' money in e-transformation, yet they have less power to stop the project and still valid explanation of programme benefits may convince them.

Agency needs to be ready to handle these kinds of human related issues. I have characterised the following key readiness criteria in this regard:

1. Leadership
2. Human resource alignment
3. Effective communication
4. Risk Management

8.2 Leadership

As we discussed earlier, lack of leadership is one barrier to the e-transformation initiative; and we discussed the importance of transformational leadership style at national and organisational level to support this endeavour.

As part of readiness assessment programme, we need to measure leadership readiness in three perspectives: awareness, embracing, and leadership skills; the interrelation of these three forms the base for measuring leadership readiness.

If leaders are aware and fully embracing e-government concepts but has ineffective leadership, then agency lacks enough leadership; on the contrary, leader owns leadership style but is not aware or is doubtful about e-government, then agency again lacks leadership and may not be able to support significant changes required by e-government initiatives.

8.2.1 Awareness

The right understanding of e-government concepts, goals, practices, benefits, and barriers, etc. is considered essential for effective leadership role; usually, national e-government programme should arrange awareness campaigns for public sector leaders to create awareness that build enthusiasm for transformation.

Audit team should assess level of awareness at agency leading team (i.e. the top leader and who directly deal with him) by interviewing leading team or filling a smart questionnaire, which asks certain questions that reflect the level of awareness.

8.2.2 Embracing

Embracement usually follows awareness but not necessarily a result of it. Successful awareness programmes should lead to a level of actions inside organisations; audit team should investigate any evidences of embracement, for example, if any activity is being arranged to introduce the idea to various managerial levels, or if any team has been devised to plan for the coming transformation, were there any initiatives that raised readiness in ICT or business process. It became obvious that these measurements are mostly subjective and based on questionnaires and interviews as data collection techniques; it need to be supported by evidences and proofed outcomes as agencies may provide inaccurate information to raise their readiness ranking while in fact they are not ready yet.

8.2.3 Leadership Skills

This is the key part of leadership readiness; if agency has enough awareness and embracement but lack leading skills, then transformation may not succeed. Leading skills are required in order to provide cultural influence and motivation to support e-government initiative at subordinates' levels as well as higher authorities (e.g. federal government).

Assessment of leading skills has various approaches and methodologies. Scholars and consulting firms had already developed many assessment questionnaires in order to measure certain traits such as vision, integrity, risk-taking/courage, interpersonal skills, communication, motivating others, empowerment, team building and team playing, individual development, result orientation, motivation ability, problem solving and entrepreneurship.

In addition to the scientific assessment, I think studying a few factors about leading team history will give some indicators as well; for example, any previous success achieved by leading team members, do they have heterogeneous backgrounds, previous exposure to serious changes in work history. Audit team should consider preparing a shortlist of leadership indications and measure it in order to evaluate leadership readiness in organisation.

8.3 Human Resource Alignment

We already discussed alignment of strategy with various resources in organisation, and already discussed alignment of business process and ICT. Human resources alignment is the complementary part of leadership and strategy readiness as e-government transformation will be conducted by agency's human resources and will directly impact them as well.

Human resources readiness will protect ICT investments in e-transformation programmes by offering higher success opportunities while reducing resistance and involving various levels of agency's staff in the initiative.

Human resources alignment as readiness criteria includes the following factors:

1. Dissemination of strategic objectives
2. Job descriptions and responsibilities
3. Policies to attract and retain skilled workers
4. HR motivation
5. HR performance management
6. HR continuous development

In the following paragraphs a brief analysis of the importance of each of the above-mentioned key points, and a suggested audit theme.

8.3.1 Dissemination of Strategic Objectives

Organisation strategy must be communicated with human resource in order to understand and participate effectively in strategy implementation. Human resource involvement exceed communicating vision and mission; real understanding of necessity to move forward in the e-transformation programme. Human resources must understand what their actual role is in the intended change. Top management should not keep workers in vague, and then they may insist on resistance and work against the project.

Clear definition of specific objectives at worker's level that results mutual benefits between management and worker is considered essential part of the balanced relationships between all stakeholders.

Without dissemination of strategic objectives, gaps will raise between management ambitions and field tasks forces; these gaps make changes to business process or ICT enablement faced by resistance due to lack of knowledge or misunderstanding.

Assessment of strategic objectives understanding could be done by selecting a random sample of workers that reflect all levels of organisation's hierarchy and expose them to a common assessment tool such as questionnaire to measure their understanding to agency objectives and strategy. Audit team may classify a set of ranks like percentage of workers who successfully define vision and mission, or number of those who successfully identify their department's unique objectives that is integrated to strategy.

8.3.2 Job Descriptions and Responsibilities

Agencies that have documented and continuously updated job descriptions for their workers will have extra readiness than those who haven't yet. Documentation will simplify implementing changes in business process and any updates in roles and responsibilities mandated by the e-government programmes.

Job description documentation is supposed to be based on identified functions and business processes; this will imply higher maturity in aligning human resources to jobs and tasks based on processes requirements. Job descriptions will also lead to easier delegation and handing over of responsibilities; even in less automated environment, documented job descriptions will help in managing authority transfer from manual system to sophisticated ones such as ERP, automated workflow, and integrated e-services.

Assessment of this criterion is straightforward; audit team just needs to assess job descriptions if such documents exist. Audit team should check its completeness, match it with existing business processes, and importantly verify the availability of effective change management for job descriptions.

8.3.3 Policies to Attract and Retain Skilled Workers

Public sector leaders should realise some barriers and risks pertaining to human resources. In order to transform agency into 'e-one', they need specialised technical and managerial skills; these skills need either to be hired, outsourced, or developed in-house by training existing staff. Enriching staff knowledge always encounters the risk of losing them unless organisation is maintaining effective retention policies.

On the other hand, employment environment in public sector including financial compensation and other benefits may not attract many skilled workers to join in; such risks put e-government programmes in jeopardy of discontinuity or incompetence.

I think such risks need to be addressed at the national level and discussed by federal government. Sharing some e-readiness initiatives between agencies may help in solving skills availability in an effective way; for example, contracting one consulting party to provide experts to serve many agencies according to needs and stage of project development.

Assessment of this criterion could be achieved by addressing these risks to agency leaders, evaluating their awareness level, and verifying any existing mitigation plans.

8.3.4 HR Motivation

Firms' leaders again should realise the risks of unmotivated human resources; simply why workers shall put extra efforts to support transformation programme! Motivation risks should be considered especially in high bureaucratic organisations.

In addition to known motivation schemes, I think motivation should be addressed at national e-readiness programmes in order to set up some common drivers at county or national level. This will be used to stimulate motivation in agencies; for example, dedicating a budget to be spent on workers show distinguished commitment, while the conventional and easier approach is to emphasise on raising interest at worker level by combining agency needs with personal human resources' development needs.

Assessment of this criterion is based on verifying and validating any motivation plans after assessing awareness level of such risks by interviewing agency leadership team.

8.3.5 HR Performance Management

Human resources performance management is another complementary readiness factor to assure that agency will be able to better manage its human capital during and after transformation. Effectiveness of organisation's services depends on the performance of the workers behind it; this will continue in the electronic age to monitor workers' performance in operating the new business processes side by side with conventional channels.

Assessment includes awareness and realisation evaluation, parallel with assessment of existing performance management systems.

8.3.6 HR Continuous Development

The importance of this criterion came from the significant need for structured training and skills development that staff is expected to experience after starting e-government programme. It will be much easier for agencies that have continuous development programmes in place to integrate e-government training requirements into their HR development system. This criterion also reflects successive management readiness which is needed to maintain business continuity and service quality.

Assessment of this factor is based on verifying and validating any development plans. Audit team can adopt a scale of four levels such as efficient, satisfactory, partially exists, and not existing.

8.4 Communication

Previously, we analysed the need for effective communication to disseminate agency strategy in order to build momentum for e-transformation programme. Communication is critically needed to effectively manage day-to-day tasks and activities and collaborating on initiatives pertaining to e-government transformation.

'People in organisations typically spend over 75 per cent of their time in an interpersonal situation' (Wertheim, 2007); this emphasises that communication is practiced most of the time in organisations.

Communication inside the organisation may have various forms. Wertheim argued five categories of communications: interpersonal, inter-group, intra-group, organisational, and external levels. In addition to that, communication is a core part of business process; for example, asking for more information, giving feedbacks and confirmations, etc., which make it subject to changes while transforming to e-government.

It is believed that agencies that practice acceptable level of communication will be more ready to afford serious changes like e-government transformation. Known project management methodologies recommended a set of best practices to utilise communication tools in order to increase stakeholders' involvement and reduce risks.

Internal organisational communication assessment may include investigating and evaluating available communications methods between horizontal and vertical managerial levels, for example, periodic meetings, reporting, follow-up mechanisms, information sharing, involvement of key stakeholders in decision making process, and possibly the ability of workers to exceed their point of contact.

8.5 Risk Management

Transformation to e-government is considered risky due to the various impacts on stakeholders and business; this justifies that agency ability to manage risks accompanying this kind of change is considered essential. In risk management there are few criteria to check. First, clarity of risk management responsibility in organisation, that is, does the top management team realise their role in managing risks? Second: are there any policies or standard for managing risks, for example, business continuity plans? If these are available, then agency will enjoy more controlled environment while transforming into e-government.

Figure 8.1 shows various changeability readiness factors.

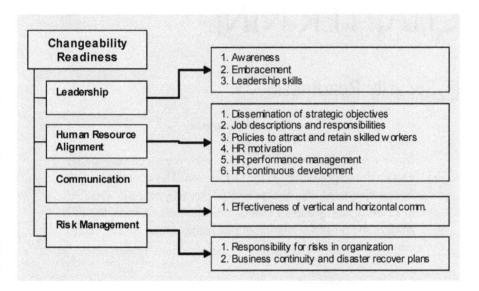

Figure 8.1: Changeability e-readiness criteria.
Source: Author.

CHAPTER NINE

IT Security Readiness

Chapter Summary

Many people think that IT security is the pure technical matter, and it's the responsibility of the IT function. This could be a myth. In this chapter, I will discuss why IT security was not classified in IT readiness group of criteria and grouped to form the fifth track of the proposed organisational readiness model. IT security contains the following sub-criteria:

1. Top management realisation and adoption.
2. Business department's readiness.
3. ICT function readiness.

W E had addressed ICT security as a major barrier to e-government; for example, privacy issues continue to be a major concern for all stakeholders. This is due to two major factors: First is the limitations in technology itself. That is part of its nature. The other is the socio-organisational factors which resulted mainly from lack of understanding of security risks and countermeasures.

ICT security have many diversified topics that are related to legal, technical, business, and behavioural issues; many parties already developed an ICT governance frameworks in order to regulate these intersecting variables. Security professionals agreed on three key objectives to be achieved by ICT security; these are confidentiality, integrity, and availability of information. In order to reduce ICT related risks in e-government programmes, these risks need to be addressed on national and organisational levels. In our e-readiness model, ICT security forms the fifth track and consists of the following criteria:

1. Top management realisation and adoption
2. Business department's readiness
3. ICT function readiness

In the following sections, I will discuss each of the above-mentioned criteria.

9.1 Top Management Realisation and Adoption

According to COBIT IV governance framework (published in 2005 by Information Technology Governance Institute), top management is responsible and accountable for all ICT risks. Leaders' right understanding for key issues and roles pertaining to ICT security is the first step in governing increasingly growing ICT risks; COBIT governance model suggests a leading role characterised by formulating a security committee to oversee and follow-up these risks, declaring a security policy statement for all staff to follow, and then it need to be augmented by monitoring mechanisms e.g. internal and external audit.

Assessment of this criterion consists of benchmarking top management realisation and activities against accepted best practices – mainly, existence of officially formulated ICT security committee, availability of current and well-communicated security policies that cover various ICT aspects, and last but not least, assessment of available compliancy inspection mechanisms.

9.2 Business Department's Readiness

Many executives think that ICT security is the responsibility of ICT function in organisation; actually, ICT security professionals agreed to segregate the roles of security into data owners and data custodians, owners are business departments according to relevancy and specialty, while ICT team play data custodians role with various levels.

ICT security implementation role is supposed to be assigned to some independent party from both owners and custodians, while it could be done form one of them under certain compensating controls. Decisions concerning ICT security should be taken in mutual cooperation between all concerned stakeholders, under the top management's vision crystallised in their security policy statement.

Assessment of this criterion is done by assessing existing situations in key business departments; do departments understand their role of data ownership? Are they involved in classifying their data and assigning security levels? How do they grant access rights for data under their ownership? And what mechanisms are used to change security settings?

Based on such information, the audit team can decide about the level of readiness of ICT security in business departments as e-transformation will require a new means for data exchange that will incur security risks usually organisations will not be ready to handle without minimum level of readiness.

9.3 ICT Function Readiness

In assessing readiness, we emphasise on agencies' realisation of the importance of best practices, parallel with assessing effectiveness of any existing practices. Audit team needs to identify a set of technical security checklists that is based on the informational model strategically adopted by agency. For example, agency informational model may include outsourcing certain tasks. This will mandate service level agreement inspection which should contain valid terms to protect agency rights and informational properties.

In general, technical security readiness should satisfy confidentiality, integrity, and availability requirements. Audit team should assess the following key criteria:

1. Realisation of technical security requirements.
2. Existing level of security practices.
3. Coordination with other departments pertaining to security.

9.3.1 Realisation of Technical Security Requirements

ICT management should understand their expected role in ICT security. My own experience revealed that many ICT departments feel purely responsible for all security roles; this lays extra burden on ICT staff and could be welcomed from other departments to keep them irresponsible for ICT security as far as ICT staff declare responsibility for this critical matter. Professional practices strongly recommend the early mentioned complementary and consistent roles between concerned parties.

Assessment also includes ICT management realisation of various ICT risks; realisation assessment includes general understanding, ability to conduct risk assessment and impact analysis study, defining follow-up and escalation procedures, and importantly, integration of security policy in internal ICT processes.

Audit team should measure these concepts subjectively and check if it's satisfactory or need enforcement since it's the key basis for healthy computing.

9.3.2 Existing level of Security Practices

Security practices were basically originated to countermeasure ICT risks. ICT risks could be a result of either nature of the technology itself, natural threats or humans who may interfere with it. ICT function should adopt a set of policies, procedures, and standards that guarantee confidentiality, integrity, and availability of information. The security standard originally known as ISO 17799:2000 based on the BS7799 that was released in 1995, and it was the bases for the ISO 27001:2005, suggests the following topics for IT security:

1. **Assets management**: defined and assigned responsibilities to protect hardware, software, and facilities.
2. **Human resources security**: control human resources risks before, during, and while ending employment (includes business users and ICT staff).
3. **Physical and environmental security**: includes power supply, fire alarms, air conditioning, preventive maintenance, physical access controls, offline facility, etc.
4. **Communication and operations management**: standard operating procedures for various devices, scheduled backup, systems monitoring, service level agreements, and network security management.
5. **Access control**: physical and logical access of users, operators, developers, etc.
6. **Information systems development, acquisition and maintenance**: include mainly definition of system development life cycle in addition to project and product quality management.
7. **Incident management**: reporting and management of various ICT events (e.g. virus attacks).
8. **Business continuity**: defined business continuity and disaster recovery processes and responsibilities.
9. **Compliancy** with any national ICT legal requirements and security policies.

9.3.3 Security Coordination With Other Departments

This criterion is to emphasise on the importance of security administration role. Audit team needs to assess level of coordination between business departments and

ICT function in agency, while implementing security policies and handling various security events.

Coordination may include normal security administration tasks, e.g. manage request to set or change access rights, it also include managing security incidents e.g. planned and unexpected downtime; such communication should be channeled via security administration role, in order to implement segregation of duties.

Finally, Figure 9.1 represents security e-readiness criteria.

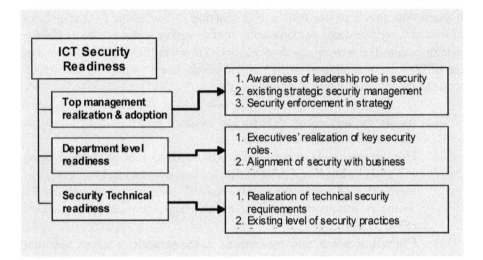

Figure9.1: Security e-readiness criteria.
Source: Author.

CLOSURE

The book was a dream. It became a reality. I started with some thoughts about e-readiness, investigation, and research in published literature thoroughly enhanced my understanding of e-readiness topic. I think e-readiness assessment will be more beneficial if conducted in a structured way. This clarifies the value behind creating an e-readiness model that contains identified criteria with specific components to be assessed at organisational level, in addition to its pertaining audit methods.

Creating e-readiness model at national level as part of e-government programme in a certain country or region will lead to a set of benefits; it could be summarised in the following points:

1. It will help in gathering and comparing different agencies' results to provide valuable information to national e-government programmes. This will increase interest and eagerness to participate at agency levels.
2. It will facilitate continuous evaluation and monitoring of advancements in various readiness criteria at agency level; structured periodic audit will keep readiness information updated and reflects current situations at agencies.
3. Structured information about readiness will help national programmes in strategic planning, monitoring progress, shortening learning curves, and optimising costs by exchanging knowledge and sharing resources between agencies.
4. National level e-readiness information will help in estimating and managing e-government programmes financially, by estimating and budgeting expected costs.
5. Finally, and importantly, it will help in coordinating efforts to reengineer shared processes in order to launch integrated e-services.

I think this model is also beneficial in assessing for-profit organisations' e-business readiness.

REFERENCES

Asia Oceania e-Business Marketplace Alliance (AOEMA) (2004). *e-government form citizen's perspectives*, a project by AOEMA presented at the Business Facilitation Steering Group meeting during Asia Pacific Economic Cooperation – Telecommunications Information Working Group summit, 2003, Malaysia. Available from: http://www.aoema.org/E-Government/ Definitions_and_Objectives.htm, Accessed 21 June 2007.

Asia-Pacific Economic Cooperation (APEC) (May 2000). *E-Commerce readiness assessment guide*, Asia-Pacific Economic Cooperation. Available from: http://203.127.220.111/query.html?qt=APEC+E-Commerce+Readiness+Ass essment+Guide, Accessed 8 May 2007.

Barton, A. H. (1979). A Diagnosis of Bureucratic Maladies. *Making Bureucracies Work*. C. H. A. H. Weiss, Burton. London, Sage.

Baum, Christopher and Maio, Andrea (November 2000). *Gartner's four phases of E-Government model*, Gartner-Group, 2000. Available from: http://www. gartner.com/DisplayDocument?doc_cd=94235&ref=g_fromdoc#top#top, Accessed 29 April 2007.

Berry, Frances (2007). 'Strategic Planning as a Tool for Managing Organizational Change' Florida, USA, *International Journal of Public Administration*, 30: 3, 331–46. Available from: *http://www.tandfonline.com/doi/ pdf/10.1080/01900690601117812*, Accessed 6 May 2007.

Berry, F.; Wechsler, B. "State Agencies" Experience with Strategic Planning: Findings from a National Survey. Public Administration Review **1995**, *55* (2), 159–167

Booz Allen and Hamilton (BA&H) (November 2005). *Beyond e-government, the most successful technology-enabled transformation*, study commissioned by UK Cabinet Office, London. Available from: http://www.boozallen.com/media/ file/151607.pdf, Accessed 30 April 2007.

Bridges.org (2002). *E-readiness assessment: who is doing what and where*, Bridges Organization, 2001. Available from: http://bridges.org/files/active/0/ereadiness_whowhatwhere_bridges.pdf, Accessed 7 May 2007.

Bridges.org (2005). *E-readiness assessment tools comparison*, Bridges Organization, 2005. Available from: http://www.bridges.org/files/active/0/ereadiness_tools_bridges_10Mar05.pdf, Accessed 1 February 2007.

Carsten, Bernd (December 2005), 'The Ethical Problem of Framing e-Government in Terms of e-Commerce', *Electronic Journal of e-Government*, 3: 2, 77–86. Available from: www.ejeg.com/volume-3/vol3-iss2/StahlBernd.pdf, Accessed 23 June 2007.

Credit Research Foundation (2007). *Glossary*, Credit Research Foundation, 2007, Columbia, Maryland. Available from: http://www.crfonline.org/orc/glossary/b.html, Accessed 11 August 2007.

Ebrahim, Zakareya and Irani, Zahir (2005). 'E-Government Adoption: Architecture and Barriers', *Business Process Management Journal*, 11: 5, 589–611. Available from: www.emeraldinsight.com/1463-7154.htm, Accessed 25 April 2007.

Evcimen, Tunç (2006). *Creativity in organizations*, Dr Tunc Evcimen website. Available from: http://evcimen.com/mis484/CREATIVITY%20COURSE%20NOTES.pdf, Accessed 4 May 2007.

Galletta, D.F.; Lederer, A.L. Some Cautions on the Measurement of User Information Satisfaction. Decision Sciences 1989, 20, 419–437; and Garrity, E.J.

Gascó, Mila (2007). 'Exploring the E-Government Gap in South America', *International Journal of Public Administration*, 28: 7, 683–701. Available from: http://www.informaworld.com/smpp/title~content=t713597261, Accessed 6 May 2007.

Harvard University (2000). *Readiness for the networked world: a guide for developing countries*, International Technology Group, Centre for International Development Harvard University, Cambridge, USA. Available from: http://cyber.law.harvard.edu/readinessguide/guide.pdf, Accessed 5 March 2007.

Health, Safety and Environment – Management Information System Web Depot Organization (HSE-MIS) (September 2001). *Glossary*. Available from: http://hsewebdepot.org/imstool/GEMI.nsf/WEBDocs/Glossary, Accessed 7 July 2007.

Heeks, Richard (2001). *Understanding E-governance for development – a framework for national and donor action*, Institute for Development Policy and Management, University of Manchester, UK. Available from: http://unpan1.un.org/intradoc/groups/public/documents/NISPAcee/UNPAN015485.pdf, Accessed 24 June 2007.

IBM (2005, 2006). *The e-readiness rankings for 2005 and 2006*, two white papers published by The Economist Intelligence Unit parallel with Institute of Business Value. Available from: http://a330.g.akamai.net/7/330/2540/20060424215053/graphics.eiu.com/files/ad_pdfs/2006Ereadiness_Ranking_WP.pdf, Accessed 4 February 2007.

Information Technology Governance Institute (ITGI) (November 2005). *Control objectives for IT and related technologies (COBIT)*, Rel. 4.0, Information Technology Governance Institute (www.itgi.org). Available from: http://www.isaca.org/AMTemplate.cfm?Section=Downloads&Template=/MembersOnly.cfm&ContentFileID=14002 (note: available for members only).

International Telecommunication Union and United Nations Conference on Trade and Development (WISR) (June 2007). 'World information society report' – third online version, International Telecommunication Union and United Nations Conference on Trade and Development, Geneva. Available from: www.itu.int/wisr and www.unctad.org/wisr, Accessed 20 June 2007.

Newcomer, Kathryn (February 2007). 'Measuring Government Performance', *International Journal of Public Administration*, 30: 3, 307–29. Available from: *http://www.ingentaconnect.com/content/routledg/lpad/2007/00000030/00000003/art00006*, Accessed 6 May 2007.

Norris, Donald, et al. (February 2001). *Is your local government plugged in? Highlights of the 2000 electronic government survey*, Prepared for the International City Management Association (ICMA) and Public Technology, Inc. (PTI), Baltimore, USA. Available from: http://www.umbc.edu/mipar/PDFs/e-gov.icma.final-4-25-01.pdf, Accessed 29 April 2007.

Office of Management and Budget (OMB), the Executive Office of USA President (2007). *Glossary*. Available from: http://www.whitehouse.gov/omb/budget/fy2003/bud35.html, Accessed 6 May 2007.

Ojo, Adegboyega, Janowski, Tomasz and Estevez, Elsa (April 2007). *Determining progress towards e-Government – what are the core indicators?* United Nations University International Institute for Software Technology, Macao. Available from: http://www.uio.no/studier/emner/jus/afin/FINF4001/h05/ undervisningsmateriale/Adegboyega-ECEG2005.pdf, Accessed 14 May 2007.

Punia, Devendra and Saxena, K.B.C. (2004) *Managing inter-organizational workflows in government services*, Association for Computing Machinery, New York, NY, USA. Available from: http://portal.acm.org/ft_gateway.cfm?id=1052283&typ e=pdf&coll=GUIDE&dl=GUIDE&CFID, Accessed 9 June 2007.

Rusaw, Carol (February 2007). 'Changing Public Organizations: Four Approaches', *International Journal of Public Administration*, 30: 3, 347–61. Available from: http://www.informaworld.com/smpp/title~content=t713597261, Accessed 6 May 2007.

Seifert, Jeffrey (28 January 2003). *A primer on e-Government: sectors, stages, opportunities, and challenges of online governance*, Report for the United State Congress, Congressional Research Service, The Library of Congress. Available from: www.fas.org/sgp/crs/RL31057.pdf, Accessed 14 May 2007.

Sudharatna, Yuraporn and Li, Laubie (2007). 'Learning Organization Characteristics Contributed to its Readiness-to-Change: A Study of the Thai Mobile Phone Service Industry', *Managing Global Transitions*, 2: 2, 163–78. Available from: http://www.fm-kp.si/zalozba/ISSN/1581-6311/2_163-178.pdf, Accessed 29 July 2007.

The Accounting Payable Network (2007). *Glossary*, The Accounting Payable Network, Atlanta, USA. Available from: http://www.theaccountspayablenetwork.com/ html/modules.php, Accessed 21 July 2007.

United Nations – World Public Sector Report (WPSR) (December 2003). *E-Government at the crossroads*, UN Public Administration and Development Division, Geneva. Available from: http://unpan1.un.org/intradoc/groups/ public/documents/UN/UNPAN012733.pdf, Accessed 30 April 2007.

United Nations (November 2004). *Global e-readiness reports – towards access for opportunity*, Department of Economic and Social Affairs – Division for Public Administration and Development Management. Available from: http:// unpan1.un.org/intradoc/groups/public/documents/un/unpan019207.pdf, Accessed 1 February 2007.

United Nations (November 2005). *Global e-readiness reports – from e-Government to e-Inclusion*, Department of Economic and Social Affairs – Division for Public Administration and Development Management. Available from: http://

unpan1.un.org/intradoc/groups/public/documents/un/unpan021888.pdf, Accessed 1 February 2007.

United Nations Commission for Europe (UNECE) (2007). *Glossary*, United Nations Commission for Europe. Available from: http://unece.org/gender/glossary/g. htm, Accessed 7 July 2007.

Wenbo, Shi (April 2002). 'The contribution of organizational factors in the success of electronic government commerce', *International Journal of Public Administration*, 25: 5, 629–57. Available from: *http://www.tandfonline.com/doi/ full/10.1081/PAD-120003293*, Accessed 12 April 2007.

Wertheim, Edward (2007). *The importance of effective communication*, Northeastern University College of Business Administration, Boston, MA. Available from: http://web.cba.neu.edu/~ewertheim/interper/commun.htm#top#top, Accessed 3 July 2007.

Wikipedia (2007). *The free encyclopedia*, various pages were carefully referred to while conducting this research.

Wyman, S.K.; McClure, C.R.; Beachboard, J.B.; Eschenfelder, K.R. Developing System-Based and User-Based Criteria for Assessing Federal Web Sites. Journal of the American Society for Information Science 1997, 34, 78–88.

APPENDICES

Appendix I – Sample e-government Model

There is no unique e-government model that best fits all nations; each country must build its own model that satisfy its e-government programme objectives and suit its national and regional readiness. Some models are more oriented towards business aiming to facilitate investments; others may seek to better serve constituents by reducing bureaucracy in government services and reduce public expenditures.

E-government model should satisfy a set of objectives. On top of it is reducing redundancy in technical components and unify exchanging information at all levels; in fact, there are several perspectives of e-government model, such as business model, technical model, and security model. Ebrahim and Irani described one model that I will consider as an example; the model was concluded based on a set of resources; it suggests a four-layer architecture that consists of

1. Access layer
2. e-government layer
3. e-business layer
4. Infrastructure layer

I will illustrate the model from bottom up as it will be easier to understand:

Infrastructure Layer

This layer includes government technological foundation; it has two major groups of components (see figure I.1):

1. Agency level infrastructure: It includes all or part of hardware and software that store and manipulate information, such as servers, network devices, databases and applications; the last contains business process logic and controls. This does not mean that any hardware or information available in agency need to be part of the e-government model or need to be shared or accessed over the common network; this assumption is one out of

many assumptions which are part of the e-government model and should be developed and revised carefully.

2. Trans-agency infrastructure: There need to be a minimum level of common infrastructure between government agencies and other key parties, such as physical and logical networked communication and access channels (e.g. Intranet, Extranet, and the Internet), common coding system, and data exchanging protocols to facilitate information sharing.

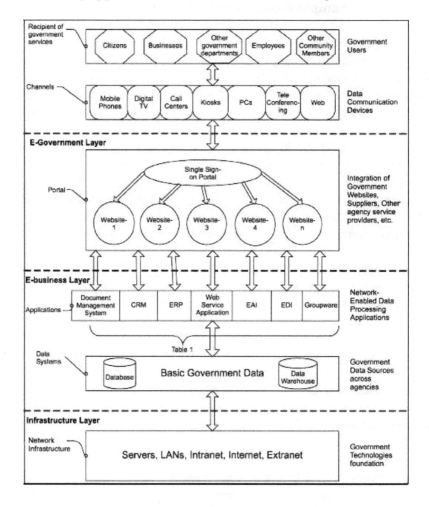

Figure I.1: Framework of e-government architecture.
Source: Ebrahim and Irani (2005).

E-business Layer

'This layer is focused on using ICT applications and tools to harness a network of trust, knowledge sharing, and information processing that takes place both within and between organisations' (Moodley, 2003, from Ebrahim and Irani, 2005); e-government implementations cannot go far beyond what this layer affords; this forms agencies' digitised knowledge base and possible utilizations of informative and transactions patterns.

Major components are summarised in the following table:

Application/system	Description
DBMS	Organisation of components that define and regulate collection, storage, management, and use of data within database environment
Customer relationship management (CRM)	Alignment of governmental business processes with citizen needs to manage and ensure they are served in logical manner and decrease costs of providing services regardless of business lines
Enterprise resource planning (ERP)	Represents business management system that integrates information flow across all functions of organisation to automate corporate business processes
Web service application	Performs encapsulated business functions ranging from simple request-reply to full business process. Government organisations can integrate a powerful, sophisticated search engine into their Internet, and Intranet environments without the need for large capital investment or substantial systems integration
Enterprise application integration (EAI)	Integrates both intra and inter-organisational systems by securely incorporating functionality from disparate applications in government organisations
Data warehousing	Essentially database that stores integrated, often historical, and aggregated information extracted from multiple, heterogeneous, autonomous, and distributed information sources
Electronic data interchange (EDI)	Electronic transfer of structured data and services using agreed message standards between computer applications
Data and knowledge management	Systemic approach to capturing information and knowledge about an organisation, its processes, products, services, customers, procedures used to conduct planning and programme evaluation in areas ranging from capital construction, to economic forecasting, to performance of school
Groupware	Collaboration tools that enable employees working in teams to share information and resources to work interactively, regardless of the physical locations of individuals, e.g. emails, notice boards, and Web collaboration

Table I-1: e-business layer components
Source: Ebrahim and Irani (2005).

E-government Layer

This layer forms the consolidated gateway for e-government services. All agencies need to be connected to this common hub to receive requests, send feedbacks, and exchange digital information between all stakeholders. Each agency need to identify its relationships with this common gateway, what electronic services they are going to offer and in what formats; for example, G2G services between agencies are to be identified, received from access layers using configured and agreed upon access modes, then passed to concerned agencies, receive feedbacks then forward it to initiator; a robust follow-up and monitoring cycle is a key success factor for e-government model.

Access Layer

This layer is used for electronic interaction between government and citizens (G2C), government and business (G2B), government and its employees (G2E), and government and government (G2G); communication channels may include Web access through Web Internet browsers, or short messaging systems (SMS). Request might be received directly from servers through the common e-government layer; receiving servers may feed back immediately of stack requests for later processing. E-government layer should provide the facility to keep requests in a queue if transaction parties are out of service.

In all layers, security in its broader means (i.e. confidentiality, integrity and availability) should be maintained in order to secure a healthy environment for e-government to prosper; this forms a real continuous challenge to all programmes globally.

Appendix II – Organisational e-readiness Summary Tables

The following tables contain summary for the proposed organisational e-readiness criteria. First column contains section number that reference criterion in the book; second column contains criterion title and a brief description about it.

Third column contains what we want to assess, and the last column contains a suggested auditing method.

Auditing methods vary between simple questionnaires to gather data that lead to a conclusion; interviews are another possible way to gather data and verify stated criterion factors.

Inspecting any provided documentation by agency is a real proof and will provide evidence about what is there and what is missing; but it needs special audit skills and reasonable understanding of criterion topic in order to fairly conclude audit results.

Table 1: Strategy Readiness Criteria

Main Criteria	Sub Criteria What to Assess	Methods How to Assess
1. **Strategic planning**	• Clearly identified and well-communicated strategic direction including vision, mission goals, strategic objectives, and programmes.	• Questionnaire • Interviews • Assessing existing plans
2. **Organisational structure (OS)**	• Availability of documented and updated organisation structure • OS is communicated and recognised by stakeholders • OS covers all strategic departments and activities, • Identified relationships and authorities • Existing mechanism to modify or enhance the structure when needed, • Job titles, responsibilities, and accountability is integrated to OS • ICT function is well positioned in order to contribute in strategic planning and execution	• Interviews • Review publications • Questionnaire
3. **Functions and services**	• Clearly defined and strategically mapped internal and external business processes • Assigned responsibilities (process ownership) • Process optimisation • Level of automation • Integration with incentive system	• Interviewing top management and key staff • Review available documentation
4. **Performance management**	• Capability of performance measurement • Any existing performance management mechanism	• Interviews • Review publications • Questionnaire • Build capability maturity model
5. **Informational Model**	*Informational model is 'a high-level roadmap containing software, hardware, and other information technology requirements for health and secured environment managed information systems' [author].* • Do existing technical model serves firms' business model? • Data requirements definitions • In-house versus outsource of needed ICT processes. • Centralised versus distributed data processing requirements • Technological directions pertaining to software, hardware, databases, and networking. • Business continuity strategy including possible disaster recovery options	• Interviewing key staff • Reviewing available documentation • Assess maturity by building maturity model.

Table 2: Business Processes Readiness Criteria

Main Criteria	Sub Criteria What to assess	Methods How to assess
6. **Documentation**	• Availability of a business process committee • Availability of updated documentation for all strategic processes • Accessibility of documentation • Availability of electronic workflow systems • Integration of BPD to human resources roles and responsibilities. • Integration of BPD to automated system.	• Interviewing key staff • Reviewing and validating relevant documentation
7. **Effectiveness**	• Clarity of process drivers, initiators, triggers, and inputs. • Clarity of process roles and responsibilities at various stages • Clarity of process exceptions and predefined handlings • Clarity of process controls and related objectives • Clarity of process outputs in various stages • Mechanisms to monitor adherence to process qualities • Level of support available at each stage	• Interviewing staff from various levels • Walking through • Sampling
8. **Performance Evaluation**	• Availability of business process performance system	• Build capability maturity model
9. **Automation**	• Level of automation of various processes tasks and steps. • Ability to integrate and exchange digital information with other stakeholders.	• Assess percentage of fully automated processes • Assess previous integration experiences

Table 3: Technology Readiness Criteria

Main Criteria	Sub Criteria What to assess	Methods How to assess
9.1 Infrastructure	• Facility infrastructure comply with informational model • Infrastructure scalability based on usage expectations of data processing and network traffic • ICT facility physical and logical security considerations • Adoption of know best practices	• Interviewing staff • Questionnaires • Walk through • Reviewing documentation • Conduct a risk based audit

9.2 Databases	• Availability of cleansed and well-structured historical information
	• Ability to share and transfer data to Web content
	• Availability counter-measures:
	  • Effective database administration
	  • Parallel replication of DBMS
	  • Licensing of concurrent users
	  • Data retention policies and backup systems
		• Interviewing ICT staff
		• Reviewing available documentation
		• Recommended to follow standard audit procedures

10. Application maturity		
10.1 Applications – functional maturity	*Level of automation or electronic processing coverage of application to the specific service or function* • Application is ready to continue servicing conventional channels of services • Application is able to segregate online services from manual ones • Application should be ready to report the status of online processed requests	• Interviewing ICT and business staff • Conducting functional test on testing environment
10.2 Applications – maintainability	*Applications are under continuous development and enhancement to reflect required changes in business logic and optimise data processing application documentation.* • Experienced resources. • License agreement that allow modification. • Effective application development and change management life cycle.	• Interviewing staff • Review available ICT policies and standards • Inspect change requests • Inspect development environment
• **Applications – integration ability**	*Exchanging digital data with existing software and hardware harmony* • Ability to integrate legacy systems with portals and Web gateways • Ability to build and operate middleware tools	• Interviewing ICT and business staff • Evaluating existing conversion tools and programmes.

Main Criteria	Sub Criteria What to assess	Methods How to assess
• **Applications – security**	*Includes a lot of factors, for example access rights, input validation and audit logs of users activities* • ICT application security model should be used (e.g. ISO27001)	• Standard Security Audit should be followed.
11. **ICT management**	• ICT function positioning in agency's organisational structure • Measure internal ICT function organisational structure comply with governance requirements • Identified and documented ICT processes (standard operating procedures) • Responsibility is assigned clearly and officially • Project management practices • ICT HR management	• Follow Standard ICT Audit Procedures and guidelines (e.g. Publications of information systems audit and control association)

12. **Technical skills**	*Various skills and talents needed in order to gain and sustain readiness to support electronic government operations for 24/7:*
	• Existing skills are satisfactory for current and future needs
	  • Project management
	  • Programming expertise
	  • Middleware and data transformation
		• Interview key staff
		• Review available documentation

Table 4: Ability to Change Readiness Criteria

Main Criteria	Sub Criteria What to assess	Methods How to assess
1. Leadership		
1.1 Awareness	*Right understanding of e-government concepts, goals, practices, benefits, barriers, etc. is considered essential for effective leadership role* • Level of awareness at agency leading team	• Questionnaires • Interviewing
1.2 Embracing	• Inspect for any evidences of embracement	• Interviews • Review existing documentation
1.3 Leadership skills	*Leading skills are required in order to provide cultural influence and motivation to support e-government initiative at subordinates as well as higher authorities Use standard leadership assessment techniques to measure leadership traits such as vision, integrity, risk-taking/courage, interpersonal skills, communication, motivating others, empowerment, team building and team playing, individual development, result orientation, motivation ability, problem solving and entrepreneurship* • Studying leading team history	• Use standard leadership assessment model and techniques • Interviews
2. Human resources alignment		
2.1 Dissemination of strategic objectives	• Human resource understanding of vision and mission, • HR understanding of necessity to e-government programme. • Human resources realisation of their actual role in the intended change	• Questionnaire • Interviews • Sampling
2.2 Job descriptions and Responsibilities	*Documented job descriptions will simplify implementing changes in business process and cater to any updates in roles and responsibilities mandated by the e-government programmes.* • Job descriptions are based on identified functions and business processes • Delegation and handing over of responsibilities • Mechanisms for updating job descriptions	• Review sample job descriptions
2.3 Policies to attract and retain skilled workers	• Many organisational development programmes suffered from losing trained workers due to ineffective retention policies. Top management awareness for these risks • Any existing retention policies.	• Interviews • Review existing documentation
2.4 HR Motivation	*Importance of developing national and organisational level motivation due to the risk of unmotivated human resources* • Any existing motivation plans.	• Interviews • Review exiting documentation

2.5 HR Performance Management	*A complementary readiness factor to assure that agency will be able to better manage its human capital during and after transformation Any existing performance management activities.*	• Interviews • Build capability maturity model
2.6 HR Continuous Development	*Streamed from the significant need for structured training and skills development agencies' staff is expected to experience after starting e-government programme any existing training strategies and activities* • Involvement of business department in identifying training needs • Involvement of workers in developing training needs • Effectiveness of successive management planning	• Interviews • Questionnaire • Review existing documentation
3. Effective communication	*Communication is needed to disseminate agency strategy and build momentum for e-government programme. It is also critically needed for effectively managing day-to-day affairs of e-government programme.* • Assess interpersonal, inter-group, intra-group, organisational, and external communications. • Investigating and evaluating available communications methods between horizontal and vertical managerial levels	• Interviews • Questionnaire • Build capability maturity model
4. Risk management	1. Responsibility for risks in organisation 2. Business continuity and disaster recovery plans	• Interviews • Questionnaire • Build capability maturity model

Table 5: IT Security Readiness Criteria

Main Criteria	Sub Criteria What to assess	Methods How to Assess
1. **Top management realisation and adoption**	• Benchmarking top management realisation and practices against accepted best practices	• Using Common ICT Governance Model, e.g. COBIT IV
2. **Business department's readiness**	• Business departments have to be involved in ICT security as data and process owners. • Implementation of segregation of duties concept • Maturity and adherence of access rights policies	• Implement accredited ICT audit programmes
3. **ICT function readiness**		
3.1 **Realisation of technical security requirements**	• ICT management should understand their expected role in ICT security existence of complementary and consistent roles between concerned parties • ICT management realisation of various ICT risks • Ability to conduct risk assessment and impact analysis study • Any existing escalation procedures • Integration of security policy in internal ICT processes	• Interviews • Questionnaire
3.2 **Existing level of security practices**	*ICT function should adopt a set of policies, procedures, and standards that guarantee confidentiality, integrity, and availability of information* • Use best practices to benchmark (e.g. ISO 27001)	• Follow standard Audit procedures for ISO 27001
3.3 **Coordination with other departments pertaining to security**	*Emphasise on the importance of security administration role* • Level of coordination between business departments and ICT function in order to implement security policies and procedures and report various security events	• Interviews • Search for evidences using standard audit process

INDEX

www.ingramcontent.com/pod-product-compliance
Lightning Source LLC
Chambersburg PA
CBHW051251050326
40689CB00007B/1156